Becoming a Movement

Radical Subjects in International Politics

Series Editor: Ruth Kinna

This series uses the idea of political subjection to promote the discussion and analysis of individual, communal and civic participation and activism. 'Radical subjects' refer both to the character of the topics and issues tacked in the series and to the ethic guiding the research. The series has a radical focus in that it provides a springboard for the discussion of activism that sits outside or on the fringes of institutional politics, yet which, insofar as it reflects a commitment to social change, is far from marginal. It provides a platform for scholarship that interrogates modern political movements, probes the local, regional and global dimensions of activist networking and the principles that drive them, and develops innovative frames to analyse issues of exclusion and empowerment. The scope of the series is defined by engagement with the concept of the radical in contemporary politics but includes research that is multi- or interdisciplinary, working at the boundaries of art and politics, political utopianism, feminism, sociology and radical geography.

Titles in Series:

Becoming a Movement

Identity, Narrative and Memory in the European Global Justice Movement

Priska Daphi

ROWMAN &
LITTLEFIELD
INTERNATIONAL
London • New York

Published by Rowman & Littlefield International Ltd.
Unit A, Whitacre Mews, 26-34 Stannary Street, London SE11 4AB
www.rowmaninternational.com

Rowman & Littlefield International Ltd. is an affiliate of Rowman & Littlefield
4501 Forbes Boulevard, Suite 200, Lanham, Maryland 20706, USA
With additional offices in Boulder, New York, Toronto (Canada), and Plymouth (UK)
www.rowman.com

Open Access to this publication was supported by the DFG funded Cluster of Excellence
"Normative Orders" at Goethe University Frankfurt am Main.

British Library Cataloguing in Publication Data
A catalogue record for this book is available from the British Library

HB 978-1-7866-0379-1

Library of Congress Cataloging-in-Publication Data Available

ISBN 978-1-78660-379-1 (cloth : alk. paper)
ISBN 978-1-78660-381-4 (electronic)

∞ ™ The paper used in this publication meets the minimum requirements of American
National Standard for Information Sciences—Permanence of Paper for Printed Library
Materials, ANSI/NISO Z39.48-1992.

Printed in the United States of America

To Ursula Daphi, in memoriam

Contents

List of Abbreviations

AC	Anti-capitalist GJM sector
ACLI	Associazioni Cristiane Lavoratori Italiani
AN	Anti-neoliberal GJM sector
ARCI	Associazione Ricreativa e Culturale Italiana
ATTAC	Association pour une Taxation des Transactions financières pour l'Aide aux Citoyens
BUKO	Bundeskoordination Internationalismus
BUND	Bund für Umwelt und Naturschutz Deutschland
CGIL	Confederazione Generale Italiana del Lavoro
CISL	Confederazione Italiana Sindacati Lavoratori
COBAS	Confederazione dei Comitati di Base
CUB	Comitati Unitari di Base
DE	Germany
EP	Eco-pacifist GJM sector
ESF	European Social Forum
EU	European Union
FAO	Food and Agriculture Organization
FG	Focus Group
FIOM	Federazione Impiegati Operai Metallurgici
G7/8	Group of Seven/Eight
GJM	Global Justice Movement
GSF	Genoa Social Forum
I	Interview
IG-Metall	Industriegewerkschaft Metall
IL	Interventionistische Linke
ILA	Informationsstelle Lateinamerika
IMF	International Monetary Fund

INT	International
IST	International Socialist Tendency
IT	Italy
KRiOPR	Komitet Pomocy i Obrony Represjonowanych
MAI	Multilateral Agreement on Investment
NAFTA	North American Free Trade Agreement
NGO	Non-Governmental Organisation
NSZZ	Niezależny Samorządny Związek Zawodowy
PCI	Partito Comunista Italiano
PDS	Partito Democratico della Sinistra
PGA	Peoples' Global Action
PL	Poland
PPP	Polska Partia Pracy
PPS	Polska Partia Socjalistyczna
PRC	Partito della Rifondazione Comunista
SAV	Sozialistische Alternative
SPD	Sozialdemokratische Partei Deutschlands
TINA	There Is No Alternative
UIL	Unione Italiana del Lavoro
UN	United Nations
UP	Unia Pracy
US	United States of America
Ver.di	Vereinte Dienstleistungsgewerkschaft
WASG	Wahlalternative Arbeit und Soziale Gerechtigkeit
WB	World Bank
WEED	World Economy, Ecology and Development
WSF	World Social Forum
WTO	World Trade Organisation
WWF	World Wide Fund for Nature

List of Illustrations

FIGURES

TABLES

Introduction

Narrating the Global Justice Movement in Europe

This spirit of the era produced ... the feeling that we could overcome these divisions ... that a common front existed. You could be moderate, you could be radical, you could be underground and you could be more institutional ... but the common ground was this idea that this world needed to be changed. Which is a very simple sentence, but in that period ... [it] was something revolutionary. (I9/IT/EP-4)

Social movements are experts in telling compelling stories. Engaged in political and cultural conflicts, social movements' central strength is to challenge existing perspectives on reality and propose new ones. Narratives play a central role in this as a good story can convince us that something is wrong, that it needs to be addressed immediately and that it requires a specific solution. A good story can also tell us who we are – as individuals and as groups.

In the past years, social movement scholars have become increasingly interested in narratives.[1] Narratives foster the mobilisation and commitment of activists as well as strengthen the resonance of their claims within public discourse and institutional politics. Their power lies in their capacity to elicit sympathy and make sense of past events (Polletta, 1998b, 2006). Movement scholars have explored the role of narratives in various contexts of contentious politics, for example, their role in compelling and sustaining collective action (e.g., Fine, 1995; Nepstad, 2001; Jacobs, 2002), in dealing with repression and defeat (e.g., Wahlström, 2011; Owens, 2009; Beckwith, 2015) or in discrediting counter-movements (e.g., Crowley, 2009).

This book explores the role of narratives in building movement identity, a vital element in activists' collective actions and continued commitment. With the 'narrative turn' in the social sciences since the 1980s, the connection between narratives and identity received considerable scholarly attention.

1

Nonetheless, this connection so far remains 'more asserted than demonstrated' (Polletta et al., 2011, p. 113) since empirical studies are rare, also within social movement studies. What qualities does a story require to build and maintain collective identity? In answering this question the book aims to contribute to a better understanding of the link between narratives and collective identity as well as of the processes underlying the formation of collective identity in social movements more generally.

My analysis in particular focuses on the case of the Global Justice Movement (GJM)[2] in Europe. Known for its geographic dispersion and diversity of groups, this transnational movement constitutes an especially striking case for studying the formation of collective identity. Its heterogeneity helps in illuminating processes of bridging differences and building commonalities across diverse sectors, also in other social movements.

The GJM concerns a cycle of mobilisations from the 1990s onwards to the late 2000s with protests against neoliberal globalisation and the growing economic, social and environmental injustice it fosters, characterised in particular by its transnational scope and its networked organisation (della Porta et al., 2006, 2007a; Rucht, 2002; Pleyers, 2010; Smith, 2001; Juris, 2005, 2008a). Later protests are understood as a new cycle of mobilisation, especially the protests against austerity measures and democratic deficits starting in Europe after 2007 in the context of the financial crisis. While there are considerable continuities between both waves, in particular with respect to addressed issues and activist networks, a shift to more national targets and tactics has been observed in the latter phase of mobilisation (Flesher Fominaya, 2015, 2017; Gerbaudo, 2016; Maeckelbergh, 2012; Císař & Navrátil, 2016).

The GJM has been described as a particularly diverse 'movement of movements' since it brought together activists around the world with very different sociocultural backgrounds and political traditions (Andretta et al., 2003; Brand, 2005).[3] Involving large trade unions as well as small environmental groups, for example, the GJM encompassed groups not only with different issue interests (e.g., work vs. environment), but also with radical as well as reformist political perspectives. Furthermore, the GJM included groups with very different organisational structures, ranging from institutionalised organisations such as trade unions, political parties and NGOs to loose grassroots networks and spontaneous initiatives.

In exploring how commonalities were constructed across this diversity in the GJM, this book aims to contribute to the considerable body of literature on the GJM in two respects in particular. First, it hopes to offer a better understanding of how activist cooperation copes with differences in political traditions and local contexts by providing new insights into the formation of GJM identity. Existing research on movement identity and specifically on the GJM identity largely focuses on activists' shared framing of problems and goals. Drawing on a rich pool of original data, the book shows that, in addition to such frames, GJM identity centrally drew on a shared narrative about its activities that provided a notion of joint experience and agency.

Second, this book contributes to existing studies through a comparative analysis of the GJM in different European countries. While several studies address GJM mobilisations in specific countries and regions, few studies systematically compare different national constellations of the GJM.[4] I intend to fill this gap by exploring the formation of GJM identity in three countries representing different constellations of the GJM in Europe: Italy, Germany and Poland. This cross-national comparison draws on the assumption that transnational movements, such as the GJM, while characterised by transnational networks, targets and framing (Tarrow, 2001; della Porta et al., 2006; Rucht, 2001), are also crucially shaped by local and national political contexts (see Tarrow, 2005; Uggla, 2006; Cumbers et al., 2008; della Porta, 2005a).[5] In analysing the formation of transnational movement identity, it is hence useful to consider national differences as well as cross-national similarities.

DIFFERENT PATHS OF THE GJM IN EUROPE

The GJM took different directions across the globe, and also within Europe GJM mobilisations differed considerably with respect to the constellation of actors and activities. The circumstances, timing, scale and composition of mobilisations significantly varied between Italy, Germany and Poland, representing different GJM constellations in Europe (see della Porta, 2007b). Regarding the composition of actors, GJM mobilisations in Italy – similar to mobilisations in France and Spain – displayed a much higher involvement of trade unions (both traditional and grassroots) than in Poland and especially Germany (ibid.). In addition, mobilisations in Germany – similar to Great Britain and Switzerland – displayed a much higher involvement of NGOs than mobilisations in Italy and especially Poland (ibid.). Furthermore, levels of mobilisation considerably differed, being much lower in Poland – as in other Central and Eastern European countries – than in Germany and especially in Italy (Piotrowski, 2017; Navrátil, 2010; Petrova & Tilly, 2007). Finally, mobilisations in Italy started earlier than in Germany, and mobilisations in Poland were last to take off.

The GJM in Italy

In Italy, the GJM consolidated and expanded in a series of campaigns and protests starting in the mid-1990s, including protests against the summit of the Group of Seven (G7) in 1994 in Naples, the Italian protests against the Kosovo War in 1999 and the protests against the WTO meeting in Seattle in the same year. Consolidation and expansion continued in subsequent counter-summits, for example, in Nice in 2000, in which several Italian activists participated. New activist networks developed against the background of political changes in Italy during the 1990s that dissolved old alliances between institutional politics, third-sector organisations and social movements and provided opportunities for new ones (della Porta & Mosca, 2008; Reiter et al., 2007). One central reason for this development was the collapse of the traditional party system in 1994 and the corruption scandals that preceded it, which considerably decreased trust in institutional politics and political parties (Reiter et al., 2007). Another reason was the weakening of the 'old left', including the turn of the successor of the communist party *Partito Comunista Italiano* (PCI), the *Partito Democratico della Sinistra* (PDS), towards more moderate (and neoliberal) goals (ibid.). Third, the government's military intervention in the Kosovo War in 1999 also strained the relations between certain third-sector organisations and parties, particularly between centre-left parties and peace groups, the latter subsequently opting for more disruptive action (della Porta & Mosca, 2008).

In this situation, new alliances were forged that built a crucial fundament for the GJM in Italy, especially the growing cooperation between third-sector associations (in particular Catholic and communist associations), social movement organisations of the 1970s and 1980s and radical grassroots groups from the environment of the *Centri Sociali* (Social Centres)[6] (Reiter et al., 2007). On top of these alliances, new actors emerged in the early 1990s that played a central role in the Italian GJM, for example, grassroots trade unions.

In contrast to other countries, trade unions constituted a leading part in GJM mobilisations in Italy, in particular the newly founded grassroots unions COBAS (*Confederazione dei Comitati di Base*)[7] and CUB (*Comitati Unitari di Base*). The more established confederate unions such as the CGIL (*Confederazione Generale Italiana del Lavoro*) and CISL (*Confederazione Italiana Sindacati Lavoratori*) became more involved only in later GJM mobilisations, especially starting from the European Social Forum in Florence in 2002 (della Porta & Mosca, 2008). Only the metalworker union FIOM (*Federazione Impiegati Operai Metallurgici*), affiliated with the CGIL, was active from early on (della Porta & Mosca, 2008).

Next to trade unions, the communist party *Partito della Rifondazione Comunista* (PRC), founded in 1991, also played a main role in Italian GJM mobilisations. While overall alliances of the GJM with parties were rare in Italy (della Porta, 2007b), the PRC developed close relationships with various groups involved in the GJM as well as with the more radical activists from the *Centri Sociali*, especially through its youth organisation *Giovani Comunisti* (Reiter et al., 2007). In addition, the PRC together with other currents from social democratic and communist parties and unions congregated around the Italian branch of *Attac* (*Association pour une Taxation des Transactions financières pour l'Aide aux Citoyens*) (ibid.). Founded in 2001, *Attac Italy* was centrally involved in various GJM activities; overall, however, it played a considerably less principle role than in Germany or France (Finelli, 2003).

Beyond the institutional left, also radical left, autonomist and anarchist activists played a major role within the Italian GJM, in particular activists linked to the *Centri Sociali* and the networks they formed, most prominently the *Tute Bianche* (White Overalls) and the *Network per i Diritti Globali* (Network for Global Rights) as well as later the *Disobbedienti* (Disobedients).[8] Both the *Tute Bianche* and *Network per i Diritti Globali* participated in the *Genoa Social Forum* (GSF), the coalition preparing the counter-summit in Genoa in 2000, though with some internal dissent (Reiter et al., 2007). The network *Tute Bianche* emerged in the late 1990s inspired by the Zapatista uprising in Chiapas (Mexico) in 1994 and involved largely activists from *Centri Sociali* in northern Italy (Juris, 2005; Membretti & Mudu, 2013). The *Network per i Diritti Globali* was formed in the context of the protests against the United Nations' Global Forum in Naples in 2001 and included activists from *Centri Sociali* mostly from Rome and Southern Italy, as well as the grassroots union COBAS (Reiter et al., 2007). After the counter-summit in Genoa in 2001, the *Tute Bianche* dissolved and relaunched in the same year in cooperation with parts of the *Network per i Diritti Globali* as the *Disobbedienti* (Mudu, 2009), a network which played an important role in subsequent mobilisations.

Another central cluster of groups with the Italian GJM were groups engaged in peace campaigns and projects in solidarity with the Global South. *Rete Lilliput* (Lilliput Network), a network of faith-based and secular peace groups as well as groups concerned with international solidarity and environmental protection, played an especially crucial role here. Launched in 1999, this network brought together a variety of groups ranging from small and local Catholic peace groups such as *Beati i Costruttori di Pace* (Blessed are the Peacemakers) to larger Catholic associations such as *Manitese* (Outstretched Hands) and parts of the Italian branch of *Pax Christi,* as well as local groups from the large Catholic workers' association *Associazioni Cristiane Lavoratori Italiani* (ACLI) (Veltri, 2003; Reiter et al., 2007). Sections of the largest left-wing cultural association *Associazione Ricreativa Culturale Italiana* (ARCI), with a long tradition in international solidarity, were also involved in the network (Veltri, 2003; della Porta & Mosca, 2008). Overall, ARCI played a crucial role in GJM mobilisations in Italy owing also to its dense infrastructure of local 'circles' across Italy. The surroundings of *Rete Lilliput* also included various environmental organisations such as *Legambiente* and the Italian section of the *World Wide Fund for Nature* (WWF) (Reiter, 2007), while the latter especially played a more marginal role in the broader Italian GJM. *Rete Lilliput* has been central to various campaigns around international solidarity and peace, including the international debt-relief campaign *Jubilee2000*.

These groups' collaborative efforts culminated in the protests against the G8 summit in Genoa in 2001. Organised by the GSF's coalition of around 800 different groups, it mobilised around 300,000 activists (Reiter et al., 2007). In the lead-up to this event, several protests against summits of international organisations took place, including the mentioned protests against the UN Global Forum in Naples in March 2001 (ibid.). The large participation of Italian activists in the Genoan counter-summit was crucially spurred also by discontent with the new centre-right government coming to power in 2001 (della Porta & Mosca, 2008). While its violent escalation triggered controversial debates about legitimate forms of protest and led to some splits within the Italian GJM, the scope of participation in GJM activities continued to grow after 2001. About a million people took part in the first European Social Forum in Florence in 2002. Participation peaked with the mobilisations against the war in Iraq on 15 February 2003 with three million participants in Italy. After 2003, joint mobilisations for global justice on this scale ceased, and the GJM in Italy localised and diversified. However, Italian activists continued to participate in various counter-summits and social forums abroad as well as in local social forums that considerably prospered from 2003 onwards (della Porta, 2005b; Reiter et al., 2007).

The GJM in Germany

Mobilisations in Germany gained strength later than in Italy (Rucht & Roth, 2008). While a first critique of international institutions developed as early as in the late 1980s – with protests against the World Economic Summit in 1985 in Bonn and against the meeting of the International Monetary Fund (IMF) and World Bank in 1988 in Berlin – it was not until the late 1990s that mobilisations for global justice took off at a larger scale (Rucht et al., 2007; Brand, 2005). Global justice networks formed and grew in the context of new political dynamics from the mid-1990s onwards, which followed a phase of stagnation and reorientation among NGOs and social movements in the aftermath of the end of state socialism. In particular, movements in solidarity with the Global South felt it necessary to reorientate themselves ideologically as they found themselves politically on the defensive since concepts of Third World and anti-imperialism seemed no longer appropriate (Rucht et al., 2007; Brand, 2005).

Developments from the mid-1990s onwards contributing considerably to the surge of the GJM in Germany included the shift of more moderate organisations, such as NGOs, towards direct action. This was largely due to negative experiences with lobbying activities and considerable successes in transnational campaigns such as the *Campaign to Ban Landmines* and the debt-relief campaign *Jubilee2000* (Rucht et al., 2007). Another development contributing to the GJM's surge was that more radical left groups, especially autonomist groups – who had been losing much of their influence in the 1980s – experienced a revival with the Zapatista uprising in Chiapas (Mexico) in 1994. Also transnational grassroots networks such as *Peoples' Global Action* (PGA), and successful transnational campaigns, such as the one against the Multilateral Agreement on Investments (MAI) in 1998 contributed to this revival (ibid.).

In general, NGOs were much more present present in German GJM mobilisations, most prominently the German branch of *Attac*, founded in 1999 by about fifty social movement organisations (Rucht et al., 2007; Brand, 2005). While at first not as dynamic as *Attac France*, *Attac Germany* rapidly grew after gaining significant public attention in the context of the counter-summit in Genoa and continued to grow and broaden its thematic scope in the following years (Rucht & Roth, 2008; Kolb, 2004). *Attac* played a main role in the German GJM since it brought together a broad scope of social and political groups, ranging from reformist to radical left groups (Rucht et al., 2007; Teune, 2012). Also a primary NGO was *World Economy, Ecology and Development* (WEED), founded in 1990, which had close ties with *Attac*.

Environmental groups and organisations along with faith-based as well as secular peace and solidarity groups form another important cluster of groups within the German GJM. Environmental groups, particularly, play a much more central role in the German GJM than in Italy and Poland. These groups range from large NGOs such as the *Bund für Umwelt und Naturschutz Deutschland* (BUND), the largest environmental NGO in Germany (part of *Friends of the Earth International)* as well as *Greenpeace*, to local and more grassroots environmental groups. Among the main faith-based groups one can also find large, established development and charity associations such as *Misereor*, *Brot für die Welt* (Bread for the World) and the German chapter of *Pax Christi* as well as more rank-and-file faith communities engaged in, for example, *Kairos Europa*, a network inspired by liberation theology. Along with faith-based groups, secular groups concerned with peace and international solidarity also played a principle role, especially the NGO *Medico International* and peace groups congregated around the *Netzwerk Friedenskooperative* (Network of the German Peace Movement). The latter became centrally involved especially in the mobilisations against the war in Iraq in 2003 (Rucht et al., 2007).

In addition to these more moderate groups, radical left, autonomist and post-autonomist groups also played a primary role in the German GJM. In the early years, especially (post-)autonomist groups were essential that were connected to the transnational grassroots network PGA, founded in 1998 inspired by the Zapatista uprising in 1994 (Maiba, 2005; Wood, 2005). A platform of internationalist groups *Bundeskoordination Internationalismus* (BUKO; Federal Coordination of Internationalism), dating back to the 1970s, was also centrally involved (Rucht et al., 2007; Brand, 2005). In later years, of the German GJM in particular the *Interventionistische Linke* (IL; Interventionist Left) was crucial, a network of undogmatic and post-autonomist groups that took shape in the lead-up to the counter-summit in Heiligendamm (Teune, 2012). While the initiative for this network had started already, earlier the network took shape only in the context of the counter-summit in Heiligendamm in 2007. Furthermore, anti-fascists and anti-racist groups were involved in GJM activities throughout the years, including various local *Antifa* groups, as well as immigration initiatives such as *Kein Mensch ist Illegal* (No One Is Illegal). Finally, groups belonging to the Trotskyist current also took part, displaying a more hierarchical organisation than the above groups, namely *Linksruck* (Left Shift, dissolving in 2007 and regrouping as *Marx21*), forming part of the *International Socialist Tendency* (IST) and the *Sozialistische Alternative* (SAV; Socialist Alternative).

While trade unions did become involved in later GJM activities, especially the service sector union Ver.di (*Vereinte Dienstleistungsgewerkschaft*), and the metal workers' union IG-Metall (*Industriegewerkschaft Metall*), they played a marginal role in the overall German GJM. The distance between social movements and unions in Germany historically is high with the trade unions traditionally close to the Social Democratic Party (SPD; *Sozialdemokratische Partei Deutschlands*) (Baglioni et al., 2008). However, with the GJM's growing focus on social policies after 2003, relations to unions were significantly improved and unions joined several protest events (Rucht & Roth, 2008).

Also, left parties played a more minor role in Germany than in Italy or Poland. In fact, relations to political parties are largely missing, with the exception of the left party *Die Linke* (The Left), a merger of the post-communist party *Partei des Demokratischen Sozialismus* (Party of Democratic Socialism) in East Germany and the West German party *Wahlalternative Arbeit und soziale Gerechtigkeit* (WASG; Electoral Alternative for Labour and Social Justice) (Rucht et al., 2007). Only the political foundations closely linked to the centre-left and left parties have continuously participated in GJM activities, especially in World and European Social Forums, and provided financial support for various activities. They include the *Friedrich-Ebert-Stiftung* (associated with the SPD), the *Heinrich-Böll-Stiftung* (associated with *Bündnis 90/die Grünen,* The Green Party) and the *Rosa-Luxemburg-Stiftung* (associated with *Die Linke*).

Overall, GJM mobilisations in Germany remained considerably smaller in scale than those in Italy. In the summer of 1999, different protests were organised against a meeting of the European Union in early June and against a meeting of the G8 in Cologne in late June with between 30,000 and 50,000 participants each (Rucht et al., 2007; Teune, 2012). While the activities were organised by different activist networks, these protests constituted a decisive first step in German GJM mobilisations, which were much more influential than the protests in Seattle in the same year that received relatively little immediate attention by German activists at that time (Rucht et al., 2007).

In the following three years, no large GJM mobilisation occurred in Germany. German activists nonetheless participated in various counter-summits and social forums abroad in this period, including the protests against the World Bank and IMF summit in Prague in 2000, the G8 summit in Genoa in 2001 and the European Social Forum in Florence in 2002 (Rucht & Roth, 2008). Large protests in Germany with about 500,000 participants took place against the war in Iraq on 15 February 2003 (Rucht, 2003). The years 2003 and 2004 in addition witnessed various local and national protests against cuts in social services (Brand, 2005), and several local social forums developed across Germany (Haug et al., 2007).

While mobilisations prior to 2007 had somewhat diversified, the protests against the G8 in Heiligendamm in 2007 considerably revived the cooperation between different left groups in Germany. Groups ranging from the radical left to NGOs worked together over months to prepare the event (Teune, 2012). Up to 60,000 people took part in various activities during the summit (ibid.). After this event, however, the broad coalition lost momentum as did large joint mobilisations for global justice.

The GJM in Poland

In Poland, levels of mobilisation against neoliberal globalisation were on a whole considerably lower than in Italy and Germany, both with respect to mobilisations in Poland and with respect to the participation of Polish activists in transnational GJM events (Piotrowski, 2017). In addition, GJM mobilisations in Poland, similar to other Central and Eastern European countries emerging from state socialism, were characterised by the prominence of subcultural and anarchist activists (Piotrowski, 2013) and low levels of cooperation between different civil society groups, especially between NGOs and social movements (Piotrowski, 2009), in the context of a 'contentious' and fragmented civil society (Ekiert & Kubik, 2001, p. 7; Ekiert & Foa, 2011).

Against this background, the rise of the GJM in Poland in the late 1990s owes less to the considerable growth of the NGO sector after transformation and the new legal opportunities and resources provided (Ekiert & Foa, 2011);[9] it was rather linked to the following two developments. First, the emergence of the GJM in Poland was connected to the politicisation of subcultural and anarchist groups in the context of the political and economic crisis of the 1990s as well as inspired by exchanges with anarchists and autonomist groups across Europe (Piotrowski, 2009, 2013). Second, the emergence and re-emergence of various socialist and communist groups in opposition to the neoliberal reforms of the transformation built a crucial fundament of the GJM in Poland (Ekiert & Kubik, 2001; Ost, 2005). Disappointed by its neoliberal policies, many activists left the 'post-Solidarity political bloc', in particular the trade union *NSZZ Solidarność* (Independent Self-Governing Trade Union 'Solidarity') and the socialist party *Polska Partia Socjalistyczna*, and these activists then formed new groups (ibid.).

Anarchist groups played a very central role in the Polish GJM in contrast to its Italian and German counterparts. Anarchist groups involved ranged from large networks such as the *Federacja Anarchistyczna* (Anarchist Federation) to several local groups and squats, most prominently the *Rozbrat* squat in Poznań. In the context of the politicisation of this scene, new groups emerged playing a principle role in the Polish GJM mobilisations, in particular anarcho-syndicalist organisations such as OZZ *Inicjatywa Pracownicza* (National Labour Union Workers' Initiative). Along with anarchist groups, radical socialist and communist groups founded in the 1990s and early 2000s also played a substantial role in Polish GJM mobilisations, especially the Trotskyist group *Pracownicza Demokracja* (Workers' Democracy) associated with the IST and the socialist group *Lewicowa Alternatywa* (Left Alternative).

Furthermore, more moderate socialist and communist groups had a considerable role in the Polish GJM, mainly small labour parties and trade unions.[10] This concerns in particular the small left parties *Polska Partia Pracy* (PPP; Polish Labour Party), *Unia Pracy* (UP; Labour United) and *Nowa Lewica* (New Left). In later years, the socialist group *Młodzi Socjaliści* (Young Socialists), founded in 2005 by activists formerly engaged in the youth organisation of the UP, was centrally involved in GJM activities. Furthermore, certain small trade unions were involved in GJM mobilisations though less centrally than the anarcho-syndicalist groups mentioned above, namely *Sierpień80* (August80), a small union linked to the PPP and *Konfederacja Pracy* (Workers' Confederation), part of the All-Poland Alliance of Trade Unions OPZZ (*Ogólnopolskie Porozumienie Związków Zawodowych*).[11]

As mentioned, NGOs played an overall minor role in Polish GJM mobilisations. Especially human rights and international aid NGOs were hardly involved in the Polish GJM, in contrast to its Italian and German counterparts,[12] as were faith-based NGOs and groups.[13] However, some small left NGOs and associations did form part of Polish GJM mobilisations, in particular the Polish chapter of *Attac* as well as other small new associations with an explicitly 'alterglobalist' agenda such as *Lepszy Świat* (The Better World) from Poznań (Piotrowski, 2017). *Attac Poland* was founded in 2001, shortly after the counter-summit in Prague in 2000. It brought together radical as well as reformist left groups in the early years, but soon lost momentum because of internal disagreements and splits after 2003.[14] While participating in various transnational GJM events, *Attac Poland* as a whole played a small role in organising and mobilising GJM protests in Poland (Piotrowski, 2017; Antoniewicz, 2012). In addition to *Attac* and *Lepszy Świat*, several left publishing projects and thinktanks also formed part of the Polish GJM, in particular *Krytyka Polityczna* (The Political Critique), founded in 2002 (Rae, 2008).[15]

Furthermore, some environmental NGOs and groups were active in the Polish GJM, primarily in later activities, such as the protests against the construction of a highway in the Rospuda Valley in 2006 or against the UN Climate Change Conference in Poznań in 2008 (Piotrowski, 2013). Environmental groups involved ranged from small, local and often more radical groups to the Polish branch of *Greenpeace* and the green party *Zieloni 2004* (renamed in 2013 to *Partia Zieloni*). In addition, some feminist NGOs and groups joined GJM mobilisations in Poland as did several artist collectives with origins in the Situationist movement of the 1960s (Piotrowski, 2017).

While the counter-summit in Seattle attracted little attention and participation, an influential event for the GJM in Poland was the protest against the meeting of the World Bank in Prague in September 2000. Several hundred Polish activists took part in this event (Piotrowski, 2017). Polish activists participated in several transnational GJM events from this point onwards, such as the counter-summits in Gothenburg and Genoa in 2001, no-border camps as well as the European Social Forums in Florence in 2002, in Paris in 2003 and in London in 2004 (Piotrowski, 2009). A range of local events additionally took place in the early 2000s, many of them related to labour struggles. Along with large MayDay demonstrations in 2001, a strike at a cable factory in Ożarów in 2002 was a prominent event that brought together trade unions, socialist and communist groups as well as anarchists (Piotrowski, 2009, 2013; Antoniewicz, 2012). Furthermore, in 2003 a number of protests against the war in Iraq brought many activists to the streets, the demonstration in Warsaw on 15 February up to 3,000 (Antoniewicz, 2012) and a total of 10,000 over the year 2003 (Shields, 2012).

The largest Polish GJM mobilisation took place in Warsaw in 2004 against the meeting of the World Economic Forum. The counter-summit mobilised around 10,000 people from anarchist, socialist and communist groups as well as environmental and feminist organisations (Antoniewicz, 2012;

Piotrowski, 2013). After 2005, broader mobilisations decreased considerably, and the participation of Polish activists in the European Social Forums also declined around 2006 (Piotrowski, 2017). However, the critique of neoliberal policies continued in several local campaigns, primarily various tenants' campaigns starting in 2004 in reaction to planned changes in tenant protection laws and gaining momentum from 2007 onwards (Antoniewicz, 2012; Domaradzka & Wijkström, 2016). Furthermore, a broad network of GJM groups organised a series of strikes and labour-related protests between 2006 and 2008, such as the demonstrations against the temporary employment agency *Impel* in Wrocław and the strike at the Budryk coal mine in Silesia (Antoniewicz, 2012; Shields, 2012).[16] Protests against the UN Conference on Climate Change in Poznań in 2008 further mobilised around 1,500 activists (Piotrowski, 2010). A Polish Social Forum in November 2010, however, found only very little resonance (ibid.).

PLAN OF THE BOOK

With its diverse national constellations of mobilisation and political traditions, the GJM requires activists to work across considerable differences. The book shows that activists' narratives played a central role in bridging the national and sectorial differences within the European GJM. Analysing diverse GJM groups in Italy, Germany and Poland, the book reveals how activists shared a specific 'GJM narrative' across countries, sectors and time – as long as they felt like part of the movement. Based on over seventy interviews and focus groups with activists conducted in 2011, 2012 and 2015 as well as on central GJM publications, I demonstrate how this narrative created a notion of shared experience and agency and how it delineated the GJM's shared cognitions, boundaries and emotional proximity. These findings contribute to a better understanding of how collective identity is formed and maintained by highlighting the interplay of identity's cognitive, relational and emotional dimensions as well as by specifying the qualities a narrative requires to foster collective identity. Furthermore, the book's demonstration of the centrality of group memories also helps comprehend movement durability and tactical decisions.

In *chapter 1* I outline the book's conceptual and analytical framework. Drawing on a socio-constructionist definition of collective identity, I argue that the gaps in existing research about movement identity, in particular its fragmentary conceptualisation and one-dimensional analysis, can be best addressed by exploring the interplay of its cognitive, relational and emotional dimensions. I reason that a narrative approach to movement identity offers the best access to this interplay. This approach has the advantage of jointly considering all three dimensions. In order to explore the role of narratives in building collective identity, I furthermore focus on group memories, that is, collective narratives about a movement's shared past, drawing from the literature on collective memory. Finally, I elaborate the book's analytical procedure that combines content and structural analyses of narratives.

Chapter 2 constitutes the first empirical chapter and compares the stories activists tell in Italy, Germany and Poland about the GJM in 2011 and 2012. First, I identify country-specific patterns in activists' narratives with respect to the events and actors considered central to it as well as country-specific patterns regarding different degrees of congruence in activists' narratives. These country-specific findings underline the significance of national and local contexts in transnational social movements. Second, I demonstrate sector-specific patterns in activists' narratives that are similar across all countries. Activists refer most prominently and most explicitly to events and groups closest to their own in terms of organisation, ideas and tactics. For example, I show that World and European Social Forums are much more prominent in narratives by more moderate activists, while more radical activists put much more emphasis on counter-summits.

Chapter 3, in contrast to chapter 2, explores the commonalities rather than differences in activists' GJM narratives. In particular, it explores commonalities in narratives across countries and sectors in order to determine the extent to which GJM activists share a group memory. I show that despite the considerable national and sectorial differences in how the GJM developed, activists share a 'GJM narrative' that integrates the different perspectives on the GJM. I demonstrate how activists order the different GJM events and experiences into a specific shared plot with a sequence of four episodes. This plot creates a sense of shared experience, of collective hardship and triumph that outlines central commonalities within the GJM with respect to cognitions, boundaries and emotional proximity. In particular the shared experience of success in overcoming neoliberal hegemony and divisions within the left – despite considerable obstacles – is highlighted. Such notion of shared experience emphasises the GJM's agency and delineates its central characteristics, underlining especially the GJM's master frame of anti-neoliberalism, its difference to previous and later movements as well as the shared feelings of disappointment and joy.

Chapter 4 examines the role of the 'GJM narrative' identified in chapter 3 in forming and maintaining collective identity. I show how closely stories and movement identity are intertwined by revealing that the GJM narrative is shared only by activists who feel part of the GJM at large. The GJM narrative hence is specific to a particular group of activists at a particular time. Comparing activists' narratives across different points in time and varying degrees of commitment, I demonstrate that activists who primarily consider themselves part of a specific GJM group or who no longer feel like part of the GJM tell different kinds of stories about the GJM. Furthermore, I reveal based on a comparison of interviews in 2011 and 2012 with central GJM publications between 1997 and 2005 that the GJM narrative had been developed and maintained by GJM activists over many years until the point when other mobilisations or engagements became more salient.

In the concluding *chapter* I summarise and discuss the book's findings on identity formation in the European GJM. I elaborate how the book's findings contribute to a better understanding of how collective identity is formed and maintained in social movements. I argue in particular that the book's insights into the role of narratives in forming collective identity provide a fruitful addition to existing research. First, the book's findings go beyond existing research's frequent focus on shared cognitions about grievances and goals by demonstrating how cognitive, relational and emotional dimensions are intertwined in the narrative formation of collective identity. The book's findings also go beyond existing studies by by highlighting the role of implicit and latent elements in identity building. Second, the findings contribute to the broader literature on identity and narrative by showing how specific kinds of narratives are particularly conducive to building and maintaining movement identity, namely group memories with a plot that allows to combine a notion of shared experience and agency with the plurality of activists' perspectives. In addition, I discuss implications of the book's findings beyond movement identity, namely with respect to movement continuity and tactical decisions. I argue in particular that the shared GJM narrative strengthened commitment and made the GJM more enduring, that it shaped movement repertoires and mediated protests' transformative effects.

NOTES

1. For an overview of the literature on social movements and narratives, see Davis (2002), Fine (2002) and Polletta (2006), and on the sociology of narratives more generally, see Polletta et al. (2011).

2. Different terms have been used to describe the movement, including anti-globalisation, alter-globalisation, alter-mondialist, globalisation-critical or no global movement.

3. In fact, because of this diversity, some scholars and activists instead refer to different global justice movements. As this book explores shared elements across this diversity, however, the term will be used in the singular – without assuming it to be a homogenous actor.

4. Prominent exceptions include the comparison Donatella della Porta offers in her edited volume about the GJM in different countries of the Global North and its

concluding chapter (2007b) as well as Grzegorz Piotrowski's comparison of the GJM in Poland, Hungary and the Czech Republic (2010, 2017).

5. On the impact of political contexts on mobilisations in Western Europe more generally, see, for example, Hutter (2014).

6. This means self-managed centres usually built in squatted buildings by radical left, autonomist or anarchist activists (see Membretti & Mudu, 2013).

7. This is understood here to include also *SLAI COBAS, COBAS Scuola* and *SIN COBAS* founded in the early 1990s (see della Porta & Mosca, 2008).

8. Not all *Centri Sociali* and all activists from each centre, of course, were involved in these networks. Activists who considered these networks too reformist were more autonomously involved in GJM mobilisations (Reiter et al., 2007).

9. Several new NGOs emerged in this period, addressing issues of, for example, human rights, democracy, international aid and environmental protection.

10. Some groups with a socialist or communist perspective are also described here as moderate because of their reformist rather than revolutionary approach and due to the degree of their institutionalisation.

11. The large trade unions *Solidarność* and *OPZZ* themselves did not engage in the GJM in Poland.

12. Various human rights and international aid NGOs exist in Poland, whose interests partly overlap with issues addressed in the GJM, such as the *Institute for Global Responsibility*, the *Helsinki Foundation for Human Rights*, the *Polish Humanitarian Action* or *Fundacja Inna Przestrzeń*. However, these NGOs largely did not consider themselves part of the GJM, nor did they become notably involved in GJM activities, as several of them also underlined in replies to my interview requests.

13. This is crucially due to the fact that Catholic organisations in Poland are strongly linked to the ruling elites (Piotrowski, 2017).

14. Disagreements in particular were focused on the issue of collaborating with right-wing groups (connected also to publications of the magazine *Obywatel*; see the following note), a debate in which activists from *Attac France* and *Attac Germany* also intervened.

15. Another publishing project that may be named in this context is the magazine *Obywatel* (Citizen). It constitutes a controversial case. While at first it published mainly articles critical of globalisation and capitalism from a left perspective, later it also published radical right-wing authors (including Horst Mahler) and most activists no longer perceived it as part of the movement (Piotrowski, 2017).

16. The network *Komitet Pomocy i Obrony Represjonowanych Pracowników* (KPiOPR; Committee for Assistance and Protection of Repressed Workers) was most active between 2006 and 2008 and included small trade unions, in particular *Sierpien80*, anarcho-syndicalist groups such as *Inicjatywa Pracownicza*, socialist and communist groups such as *Pracownicza Demokracja* and *Młodzi Socjaliści*, anarchist activists from the *Federacja Anarchistyczna* as well as the alter-globalist associations *Attac* and *Lepszy Świat* (Antoniewicz, 2012).

Chapter 1

Movement Identity, Narrative and Memory

Since the 'cultural turn' in social movement studies, collective identity has been a central theme in research about political activism. Collective identity is widely understood as constitutive of social movements since activists' collective actions and continued commitment depend on the commonalities they recognise among each other.[1] Moreover, collective identity is considered a concept that allows insights into movement dynamics that other approaches to social movements left largely unaddressed, in particular resource mobilisation and political process models owing to their structural and instrumental focus. This concerns especially the questions how collective actors and interests emerge and what motivates collective actions and strategies beyond calculations of costs and benefits (Polletta & Jasper, 2001; Flesher Fominaya, 2010a). Accordingly, collective identity is frequently drawn upon to explain a variety of movement dynamics, including the emergence, trajectories and outcomes of movements.[2]

The frequent use of the term, however, stands in stark contrast with its fragmentary conceptualisation (Rucht, 1995; Daphi, 2011). Francesca Polletta and James Jasper (2001) similarly argue that 'collective identity has been forced to do too much analytically', leaving key questions about how collective identity is formed unanswered (p. 284). In this way, studies often take the existence of collective identity for granted rather than exploring its formation empirically (Hunt & Benford, 2008). Furthermore, I argue that studies that *do* examine the construction of movement identity tend to focus on either its cognitive or emotional dimension, neglecting the interplay of these dimensions.

With the aim to provide a more comprehensive insight into collective identity formation, this book analyses the interplay of cognitive, relational and emotional dynamics of identity formation by drawing on a narrative approach. Focusing in particular on collective narratives about the move-ment's past, the analysis sheds light on connections between identity, narra-tive and memory and brings together the recently growing strand of research on narratives with that on memory in social movements. The following outlines the book's conceptual and analytical approach, first defining col-lective identity as a group characteristic constructed in social interaction , which outlines shared cognitions, social boundaries and emotional proximity. Second, I argue that a narrative approach to movement identity is particularly conducive to jointly considering collective identity's cognitive, relational and emotional dimensions. Third, I add detail to the book's focus on a particular type of narrative, 'group memories', that is, collective narratives about a group's history, drawing on the literature on collective memory. Fourth, I propose an analytical procedure that combines content and structural analysis of narratives. Finally, I present the data drawn upon in this book.

COLLECTIVE IDENTITY IN SOCIAL MOVEMENTS

Movement identity refers to the collective identity of a social movement. In contrast to individual and social identity, collective identity concerns the *definition of a collective as a group with certain commonalities that members ascribe to it in interaction.* This book hence considers collective identity as socially constructed (Blumer, 1969; Berger & Luckmann, 1991). This means that commonalities are not simply a matter of preexisting similarities (e.g., personal dispositions) or objectively shared interested, but are actively and continuously constructed and reconstructed in social interaction (Melucci, 1989, 1996; Taylor and Whittier, 1992; Hunt et al., 1994; Rucht, 1995; Eder, 2000; Flesher Fominaya, 2010a). The formation of collective identity thus involves considerable efforts in meaning making,[3] in so-called identity work (Snow & Anderson, 1987). Such 'identity work' takes place in continued interactions that actors engage in individually and collectively construct-ing commonalities in relation to other actors, including opponents (Snow & McAdam, 2001). 'Imaginations about commonalities' (Jasper & McGarry, 2015), hence, are continuous 'interactional accomplishments' (Hunt & Benford, 2008).

Furthermore, this book – contrary to other publications on movement iden-tity[4] – locates collective identity at the group level (Melucci, 1996; Gamson, 1992; Flesher Fominaya, 2010a) rather than the individual level: Collective identity is understood to refer to the characteristics of a group rather than individuals' qualities or connections to the group. In this vein, collective identity goes beyond the sum of individual identities and identification processes and constitutes a social fact *sui generis* (Durkheim, 1965), a set of shared meanings that influences social action (Billig, 1995; Eder, 2009; Johnston et al., 1994). As such, collective identity also differs from social identity since it is constitutive of groups: members of the group are not only determined externally as such, but actively share and formulate commonalities (Rucht, 2011). Hence, while related, personal, social and collective identities concern different levels of identity work.

What does collective identity consist of? What are its central 'ingredients' (Daphi & Rucht, 2011)? There are various distinctions between collective identity's different dimensions (e.g., Taylor & Whittier, 1992; Hunt & Benford, 2008). I draw an analytic distinction between three dimensions – shared cognitions, social boundaries and emotional proximity. This combines Alberto Melucci's seminal distinction between collective identity's cognitive, relational and emotional dimensions with Verta Taylor and Nancy Whittier's (1992) influential conceptualisation of movement identity.[5] Cognitive, relational and emotional dimensions of identity formation, of course, overlap empirically; for example, social boundaries may draw on differences in cognitive definitions or feelings of anger. However, their distinction provides a useful analytical tool to understand different elements of identity formation.

First, a shared outlook on the world is crucial in defining a collective as a group since an outlook defines the group's ends, means and field of action (Melucci, 1996). Such *shared cognitions* include what Taylor and Whittier (1992) define as consciousness: 'the interpretative frameworks that emerge out of a challenging group's struggle to define and realize its interests' (p. 111). Shared cognitions hence are malleable; they are continuously negotiated and renegotiated (della Porta et al., 2006). They centrally include diagnostic and prognostic frames, that is, shared views on relevant issues, sources of problems and solutions (see details in the next section), but they may also go beyond these kind of frames and encompass ideologies and normative beliefs (Eder, 2011).

Second, collective identity formation is embedded into a 'network of active relationships' (Melucci, 1996), which draws *social boundaries*.[6] Social boundaries are crucial to forming collective identity as the image of 'the other' serves as a point of reference for one's own group (Taylor & Whittier, 1992; Rucht, 1995; Gamson, 1997; Eder, 2011; Tilly, 2002). This draws on Alain Touraine's (1977, 1981) seminal argument that conflict with another group is constitutive of social movements. The perceived similarity of a group essentially draws on the continuous contrast between 'us' and 'them', between the outside and inside. The 'others' may concern a variety of actors ranging from the movement's adversaries to other movements. Internal differentiations may also play a role, for example, signalling differences in the coherence of 'our' group versus 'theirs' (see Daphi, 2014a, 2014b).

Third, construction of commonality draws on *emotional proximity*. Melucci (1996) points out that collective identity requires 'a certain degree of emotional investment', which facilitates feeling like part of a community (p. 80). In this vein, some scholars highlight that the strength of an identity comes from its emotional side (e.g., Goodwin et al., 2001). Among activists' broad spectrum of individual emotions, I argue that emotional proximity in particular is crucial to movement identity. Emotional proximity refers to the shared feelings of closeness within and distance to the outside and includes what James Jasper (1998, 2014) defines as reciprocal and shared emotions on a group level. Reciprocal emotions concern people's ongoing feelings towards each other, including feelings such as trust and admiration but also envy and resentment. Shared emotions in contrast are short lived and context specific, occurring in reaction to external factors (e.g., the police blocking the road) and include fear, surprise, anger, disgust, joy and sadness (Jasper, 1998, 2014). For collective identity formation, both sets of feelings gain their power from being expressed jointly, relived in rituals and recognised as shared (e.g., collective outrage).

Beyond sharing these three dimensions, movement identity, of course, takes different forms within each movement. Collective identity may be more concrete or abstract (e.g., Rucht, 1995), more open or more closed (e.g., della Porta, 2005a), as well as more contested or consensual (e.g., Holland et al., 2008; Barnes, 2015). Large and heterogeneous movements such as the Global Justice Movement (GJM) have been observed to base on a movement identity that in contrast to others is more open in terms of being tolerant to differences and more broad in terms of defining general but not all-encompassing commonalities (see e.g., della Porta, 2005a; Daro, 2009; Flesher Fominaya, 2010b; Daphi, 2014b). The overall movement identity hence in these cases coexists with several group-specific identities. While the form that collective identity takes in heterogeneous and networked movements may be more inclusive and fluid, collective identity here nonetheless remains a crucial factor in fostering joint action.[7] These movements' tolerance of differences does not relieve us from answering the question how commonalities are defined; on the contrary, it makes this question all the more pressing.

DIFFERENT APPROACHES TO COLLECTIVE IDENTITY

Three different approaches can be distinguished within existing empirical studies of movement identity: frame analysis, collective enactment and narrative approaches (see also Daphi, 2011). While each approach offers unique insights into the processes of forming movement identity, I argue that particularly the first two tend to focus on either cognitive or emotional dimensions of collective identity. While all approaches consider collective identity's relational dimension to a certain extent, empirical studies employing frame analysis primarily focus on identity's cognitive dimension; and those following enactment approaches mostly focus on emotions. Narrative approaches, in contrast, address the interplay of relational, cognitive and emotional dimensions to a larger extent. In order to provide a comprehensive insight into all three dimensions of collective identity formation, this book hence draws on a narrative approach.

Frame Analysis

The majority of empirical research on movement identity focuses on activists' framing; this is the case in early studies (e.g., Snow et al., 1986; Snow & Benford, 1992; Tarrow, 1992; Gerhards & Rucht, 1992) as well as more recent research (e.g., Ferree et al., 2002; Andretta et al., 2003; Payerhin & Zirakzadeh, 2006; Dufour & Giraud, 2007; Tucker, 2013; Kern & Nam, 2013). Frame analysis constitutes a well-developed and prominent approach in the literature on social movements overall. Drawing on Goffman (1974), frame analyses focus on activists' interpretative schemata that simplify and condense the 'world out there' (Snow & Benford, 1992, p. 137). Particular attention is paid to those schemata that identify problems and their causes (diagnostic frames) and specify countermeasures in terms of targets and strategies (prognostic frames). Such shared frames help activists make sense not only of their environments but also of themselves as a movement. Frames proffer, reinforce and elaborate movement identity by attributing characteristics to the movement.

Frame analysis is also very prominent in existing research on the formation of collective identity in the GJM. Donatella della Porta, Massimiliano Andretta, Lorenzo Mosca and Herbert Reiter (2003, 2006),[8] for example, show how a GJM identity 'in the making' drew on a shared 'master frame' condensing the groups' different diagnostic and prognostic framing. Within this master frame, the groups' differing micro-interpretations (e.g., international solidarity, communist anti-capitalism) were merged into a shared definition of the problem (neoliberal globalisation) of culprits (international organisations such as the World Bank as well as multinational corporations) and of countermeasures (central among them being the globalisation of social rights).

Collective Enactment

Studies focusing on collective enactment emphasise that holding shared views and goals alone is not sufficient for the construction of collective identity; that is, these shared views and goals need to be enacted collectively (see also Rucht, 1995). Scholars of collective enactment argue that while talk is an important resource, it is somewhat less effective in cementing loyalty and a sense of community than is physical action in a public domain, especially if it is emotionally charged and ritualised (e.g., Jasper, 1997; Haunss, 2004, 2011; Juris, 2008b; King, 2003; Flesher Fominaya, 2007, 2010b).

Studies following the collective enactment approach have increased in recent years, and they focus either on actions of everyday life (e.g., Taylor & Whittier, 1992; Haunss, 2004, 2011; Taylor & Leitz, 2010) or on extraordinary actions – mainly protest experiences (e.g., Jasper, 1997; Juris, 2008b; Russo, 2014). In spite of the differences between extraordinary and everyday experiences, both strands of studies within the collective enactment approach share the Durkheimian (1965[1912]) emphasis on the role of ritual actions in bodily co-presence for maintaining emotionally charged boundaries that define movement identities (Aminzade & McAdam, 2001; Collins, 2004). For example, Sebastian Haunss's (2004) study of the German autonomist and gay movements shows how practices of everyday life in movement 'scenes' facilitated the construction of collective identity (see also Leach & Haunss, 2008). With respect to extraordinary activities, for example Jeffrey Juris (2008b) reveals in his study of the GJM's counter-summits in Prague (2000) and Barcelona (2002) how the protests' complex ritual performances and 'techniques of the body' – including occupying urban space, rhythmic dancing and violent confrontations – triggered emotions that strengthen activists' solidarity and generate alternative identities.

Narrative Approaches

Studies following narrative approaches focus on the role of telling stories in building movement identities. While some early publications on movement identities mention stories (e.g., Snow & Anderson, 1987; Snow & Benford, 1988; Hunt et al., 1994; Hunt & Benford, 1994; Melucci, 1996), it is only more recently that the narrative formation of movement identity has been explored more systematically in empirical studies (e.g., Polletta, 1998b, 2006; Fine, 1995, 2002; Nepstad, 2001; Guzik & Golier, 2004; Jacobs, 2002; Steward et al., 2002). Beyond research on social movements, various studies explore the role of narratives in building collective identity, for example, with respect to ethnic identity (e.g., Prins et al., 2013; Smith, 2007; De Fina, 2003, 2006; Anthias, 2002; Cornell, 2000), class identity (Steinmetz, 1992; Somers, 1992), national identity (Kane, 2000; Hart, 1992) or European identity (Eder, 2006; Crolley & Hand, 2006).

Drawing on the classic literature on narration and identity (e.g., White, 1981; MacIntyre, 1981; Ricoeur, 1984; Carr, 1986; Polkinghorne, 1988; Somers, 1992, 1995, 1994), narrative approaches to movement identity consider narratives as constitutive of identity. Narratives play a crucial role in how movements make sense of the world and of themselves (Fine, 1995; Polletta, 1998a, 1998b, 2006; Davis, 2002; Eder, 2011). This is how narratives are not only a medium of representing 'something that already exists independently', but also actively shape reality constituting 'the community, its activities, and its coherence in the first place' (Carr, 1986, p. 126).

The central role of narratives in forming collective identity is attributed to their particular qualities in representing and shaping social reality. Scholars in this context stress that narratives or stories[9] not only represent events, but also order them into a meaningful sequence, 'emplotting' them into 'evolving wholes' (Somers, 1994; Polletta, 1998a). The literature on narration and identity defines the sequence into which events are ordered, that is, the plot,[10] as a defining characteristic of narratives (Davis, 2002). Accordingly, this literature emphasises that narratives – in contrast to other forms of representing social reality – are temporally constitutive as they order events into sequences with a beginning, a middle and an end. This temporal dimension of narratives provides important clues about interpretations of causes and effects – for example, by describing what came first (a trigger) and what came after (a result) (Chatman, 1989). The temporal ordering of narratives as Francesca Polletta stresses (1998a, 2006) is what distinguishes them from frames which 'create meaning through analogy and difference' (Polletta, 1998a, p. 422), and neglect the temporal dimension (see also Sewell & McAdam, 2001).

In the same vein, Polletta's research about U.S. student sit-ins in the 1960s (1998b, 2006) reveals how a new collective identity of student activism was created based on a shared narrative of the mobilisations being spontaneous. In this shared narrative, activists delineated the boundaries of their movement by presenting themselves as spontaneous protestors. This helped distancing themselves from other approaches to protest: first, from the gradualism of prior Black protest forms (spontaneity denoting urgency); second, from the incomplete engagement of adult leaders (spontaneity denoting moral imperative to act); and third, from the hierarchy and bureaucracy of existing organisations (spontaneity denoting local initiative and independence from other left-wing groups).

This book follows such a narrative approach to collective identity since it allows insights into the interplay of the cognitive, relational and emotional dimensions of forming collective identity to a larger extent than the other two approaches.[11] As shown above, frame analyses of identity formation primarily focus on the role of shared cognition, analysing shared views of problems and goals; enactment approaches largely focus on emotional proximity. Drawing on a narrative approach, the book's central point of departure is that activists determine which shared cognitions, social boundaries and emotional proximities are relevant to their movement in and through certain narratives.

Of course each element can also exist independently of narratives; however, these elements are reinforced when woven into a narrative. Hence, if connected to a notion of shared experiences, shared cognitions, social boundaries and emotional proximity attain greater relevance to commonalities.

First, narratives express and shape shared cognitions – in both explicit and implicit forms. For example, the analysis of a problem and a solution to it may be highlighted through recounting a certain sequence of events (e.g., first the rainforest was pristine and diverse; then it was destroyed). Narratives encompass such shared cognitions in terms of both explicit arguments about the way in which problems are analysed and solutions are sought – as often analysed in frame analyses – and in terms of implicit and less reflected elements of a movement's meaning making, its 'hidden patterns' (Ricoeur, 1991, p. 482). Paying attention to such implicit shared cognitions along with explicit frames is crucial because there may be latent elements so evident that they are not part of explicit framing (see e.g., Flesher Fominaya, 2014; Polletta, 1998a; Rucht, 1995; Fine, 2002).

Second, narratives express and shape emotional proximity. Emotions are central to the process of narrative comprehension as narratives are shared empathically (Eder, 2006; Lehnert & Vine, 1987). Some sociologists in this vein even argue that emotional experiences are accessible only in narrative form (Kleres, 2011; Bamberg, 1997). The recounting of actions draws out strong emotional responses such as sympathy and anger thanks to stories' 'personal immediacy and symbolically evocative renderings of experience' (Davis, 2002, p. 24). This allows audiences to share an affective state as well as identify with protagonists, especially if events are presented as common experiences (Fine, 1995; Polletta, 1998a, 2006). In this way, shared emotions experienced during protest events (e.g., joy) can be relived and reproduced through narratives (see e.g., Jasper, 1997). Gary Alan Fine (1995), for example, shows how different movement stories produce sympathy for the teller and anger at the culpable. 'Horror stories' of past suffering and injustices and 'war stories' of mobilisation may provoke disgust and anger, desire for action or increased commitment (Fine, 1995, 2002).

Third, narratives express and shape social boundaries (Tilly, 2002; Hunt et al., 1994). Activist narratives not only identify and characterise the movement's central actors and events, but also delineate the movement's commonalities by distancing the movement from other actors. The study by Francesca Polletta (1998b, 2006) discussed above shows this very clearly, revealing how student activists centrally characterised their movement through narratives of spontaneity that distinguished themselves from previous movements. By drawing boundaries to the 'others', narratives emphasise the characteristics of the own movement as also other studies show (e.g., Guzik & Golier, 2004; Daphi, 2017).

NARRATIVE IDENTITY FORMATION AND GROUP MEMORY

As the book's introductory chapter elaborated, the literature on narratives in social movements has been growing significantly in the past few years. Despite this growth, the link between movement identity and narratives is understudied. In particular, it remains unclear what kind of narrative fosters movement identity. Also studies on narrative identity formation beyond social movement studies disagree about the most effective kind of story in this regard. While some stress the centrality of coherent narratives integrating different accounts into one story that underlines the unity and agency of the group (e.g., Carr, 1986; Steinmetz, 1992), others doubt the centrality of coherence and instead stress the role of shared overarching themes (e.g., Cornell, 2000; Prins et al., 2013) and interpretational openness (e.g., Polletta, 2006; Polletta et al., 2011). This disagreement often has to do with the fact that studies examine different kinds of narratives when exploring processes of building identity. In particular, while some studies focus on collective narratives, others focus on individual ones. This is also the case within social movement studies, as I will elaborate below. The majority of studies focus on the role of individual narratives or collective narratives of external events in building movement identity. This book, in contrast, focuses on collective narratives activists tell about the movement itself, so-called group memories, drawing on insights from memory studies.

Narratives in social movements are diverse and need not necessarily be relevant to collective identity building. A number of studies, for example, focus on *personal narratives* and how they induce political mobilisation. These include 'self-narratives' (Davis, 2002) that precede involvement in the movement such as life stories (e.g., Brown, 2002; Rice, 2002) or traumatic personal experiences, for example, with respect to violence against women (e.g., Rothenberg, 2002) or harassment (Dimond et al., 2013). Personal narratives encompass also stories about individual experiences of participating in the movement. With respect to stories preceding mobilisation, Gary Alan Fine (1995), for instance, shows how the 'horror stories' of victims raised awareness of injustices and compelled collective action in the context of the Minnesotan social movement organisation called Victims of Child Abuse Law. With respect to individual stories of participation, some studies show how such narratives contribute to building collective identity as they strengthen solidarity and identification with the movement and draw boundaries (e.g., Steward et al., 2002; Guzik & Golier, 2004). Gary A. Steward and his colleagues (2002) in this vein describe how participant narratives in a U.S. metaphysical movement helped to build collective identity by delineating antagonists and creating collective consciousness.

On the other hand, narratives in social movements can also concern *collective narratives* or so-called 'movement narratives' (Benford, 2002). These include collective stories about developments both internal and external to the movement. With respect to external stories, for example about 'domains of the world the movement seeks to change' (Benford, 2002, p. 54), a number of studies show how they contribute to building collective identity by strengthening solidarity among activists and fostering identification with the movement and the issues it raises (e.g., Farthing & Kohl, 2013; Nepstad, 2001). This is the way in which Sharon Nepstad (2001) shows how the painful martyr story of a Salvadoran Archbishop in the 1970s contributed to building a transnational movement identity in the U.S. and Central American peace movement of the 1980s.

Collective narratives, however, can also concern 'group memories', that is, stories members tell about themselves as a collective and their past joint activities. Movement scholars explore a variety of such stories, for instance stories of success such as Fine's (1995) 'happy endings' (at the collective level) and the narrative of spontaneity by the student activists in Polletta's research (1998b, 2006). Robert Benford (2002) similarly describes the U.S. peace movement's 'myth' about the effectiveness of its non-violent resistance and grassroots organisation. Scholars have also examined group memories of defeat, such as in the Amsterdam squatters' movement (Owens, 2009) or the labour movements in Great Britain and the United States (Beckwith, 2015). Few of these studies, however, systematically address the question of how such group memories affect movement identity (exceptions include: Polletta, 1998b, 2006; Guzik & Golier, 2004).

To address this gap, this book explores the role of group memories in building movement identity. Analyses of the narrative formation of collective identity can considerably profit here from studies on collective memory due to their emphasis on a shared past and collective stories. The literature on collective memories has shown in various contexts how crucial collective narratives about a shared past are to collective identity building as they provide a sense of cohesion and continuity of the group over time (Halbwachs, 1980[1950]; on national identity, see e.g., Zerubavel, 1995; Calhoun, 1997; Smith, 1999; Aguilar Fernández & Humlebaek, 2002). In addition to drawing attention to the role of a particular content of narratives (shared past), this literature underlines the collective dimension of forming movement narratives: As Maurice Halbwachs (1966[1925]) has famously emphasised, all remembering takes place in groups and is therefore shaped by particular social settings. Interpretations of past events hence are formed in present social interactions that integrate various pasts into 'a common past that all members of a particular community come to remember collectively' (Zerubavel, 1996, p. 294), a memory that 'speak[s] in the name of [a] collectivity' (Olick, 1999, p. 345).[12] This means that interpretations of past events are subject to group dynamics, including power constellations, conventions of commemoration (e.g., Olick & Levy, 1997; Jansen, 2007) and conflicts (see e.g., Bosco, 2004; Doerr, 2014b).

The book's point of departure hence is that collective narratives about a shared past are particularly central to building collective identity. In contrast to personal stories of suffering or empowerment and also in contrast to collective stories of events external to the movement, such collective narratives outline the movement's shared history. This creates a notion of shared experience that is central to defining commonalities and attributing agency to the movement. While personal stories of empowerment, for example, can of course contribute to the formation of such group memory (see Guizik & Golier, 2004), when and how they do so remains an empirical question and cannot be taken for granted.

The book's emphasis on group memories in narrative identity formation brings together two recent strands of research within social movement studies: In addition to the growing interest in narratives, movement scholars have become increasingly interested in the role of collective memory in social movements (e.g., Armstrong & Crage, 2006; Harris, 2006; Jansen, 2007; Gongaware, 2011; Daphi, 2013; Zamponi & Daphi, 2014; Doerr, 2014a; Zamponi, 2015; Baumgarten, 2016). While both strands of research use the terms *memory* and *narrative*, their approaches remain different and somewhat unconnected. The book connects both strands, in particular the memory studies' emphasis on the formation of a collective past with the narrative studies' emphasis on narrative structures. The book in this vein not only contributes to existing studies on narratives in social movements thanks to its focus on the often neglected collective narratives about past movement activities. It also adds to studies on memory in movements due to its attention to the form in which past events are told, that is to narrative structures. Narrative structures are often neglected in existing studies on memory in movements as they largely use the term *narrative* to refer to specific themes of memories (e.g., 'narratives of motherhood') rather than to specific narrative structures. Of course, the collective narratives examined in this book refer to a particular way of remembering a group's past that covers only one 'channel' of commemoration. Other 'sites' and practices of memory include, for example, memorials, photographs, rituals and symbols (Zerubavel, 1996; Erll & Rigney, 2009).

COMBINING CONTENT AND STRUCTURAL ANALYSIS

Stories encompass particular elements which are important when exploring the narrative formation of collective identity. Narratives share some structural elements that to a certain extent are transposable between different contexts and groups (Polletta et al., 2013). Classical narratologists in this vein identify

universal narrative structures with respect to plot and character constellation (e.g., Todorov & Weinstein, 1969; Barthes, 1975; Labov & Walestzky,
1967; Levi-Strauss, 1963).[13] Semiologist Algirdas Julien Greimas (1970), for
example, identifies six central actants (a receiver and a sender, a hero and an
object, a villain and a number of helpers) and their crucial functions within
narratives. And the Russian folklorist Wladimir Propp (1968[1928]) identifies a typical sequence of seven episodes with thirty-one different 'functions'
of narratives (e.g., complicity, departure, exposure).

While cautious about the universality of such structures, studies of the
narrative formation of movement identity emphasise in particular the role of
plots, as elaborated in the previous section. Meaning making in narratives
bases itself centrally on the temporal order into which events are placed as
it selects and evaluates events (Jacobs, 2002). Hence, events in narratives
are linked not only by chronology, but also by plots transforming a 'mere
succession of events' (Ricoer, 1984, p. 65) into an unfolding meaningful
story (Polletta, 2006; Davis, 2002). A minimal, shared definition of plots is
that they portray events in a sequence with a beginning, a middle and an end
(Davis, 2002). Not only is the beginning the first of a series of events, but
from it follow all the subsequent events, and protagonists here often face a
challenge. The middle contains a turning point that, to some extent, reverses
the initial situation. And the end brings a closure to the events set in motion
by the beginning; however, not all stories fully provide such closure (see e.g.,
Benford, 2002; Brown, 2002).

Such plots can be interpreted and analysed in different ways. Movement
scholars analyse plots mainly in terms of various major themes of movement
narratives drawing on classical literary 'genres' such as tragedy and comedy
(White, 1981; Ricoer, 1984).[14] Similarly, Fine (1995, 2002) distinguishes
between activists' personal 'war stories', 'horror stories' and 'happy endings'. Also Ronald Jacobs and Philip Smith (1997) emphasise the role of
romantic and ironic plots in social movements. In this book, I will instead
explore plots more in terms of the specific order in which events are retold
drawing on structural approaches to narrative analysis developed outside
social movement studies.

Beyond the study of social movements, some influential recent studies
focus on structural patterns within their narrative analysis of identity formation, looking at the form and context in which events are retold (e.g.,
Bearman & Stovel, 2000; Smith, 2007). Focusing on the form and context
in which events are retold, these scholars draw on the assumption that by
identifying only certain recurrent themes, the original story is often recom-
posed 'with the coherence and context of each original narrative lost and
forgotten' (Franzosi, 1998, p. 548). In this vein, Peter Bearman and Katherine
Stovel investigate the role of Nazis's autobiographical stories in individual

identity formation, focusing on the 'narrative network', that is, the ways in which events are linked. They show how stories relevant to identity formation contain dense cognitive links between events through 'cognitive clauses' that reconstruct the becoming of an actor with a causative structure and a high degree of self-reflection. Tammy Smith (2007) similarly shows how Italian and Croatian Istrians in New York, formerly in conflict, were able to form a joint Istrian identity through sharing certain structural elements in their narratives, namely by building new cognitive links between certain events and omitting previous controversial links.

Drawing on both strands of narrative analysis, this book will combine structural and content analysis of activists' narratives, especially in chapters 3 and 4. In particular, the analyses will distinguish between the order in which events are recounted and the characteristics, meanings and consequences attributed to these events. Scholars have used different terms to distinguish between these two levels of meaning making in narratives, for example, between story and narrative discourse (Chatman, 1989) or between distributional and integrative elements (Barthes, 1975). In this book I refer to these different levels of narrative meaning making as *events* (i.e., sequences of single actions) and *evaluations*. Evaluations concern the specific reflections about an event, often used by a narrator to connect different events (e.g., 'those were tough times'), and include cognitive, emotional as well as moral interpretations. Events, hence, are connected not only through the order in which they occur and the context in which they are placed, but also through specific meanings attached to them.

Data

The book's analysis draws on a rich pool of original data that provides crucial insights into the connection between collective narratives and movement identity. In particular, data has been collected at different points in time and with respect to a diverse range of GJM activists allowing to compare GJM narratives across time and different degrees of activists' commitment.

In accordance with the analytical approach outlined in the previous sections, the book explores activists' collective narratives about the GJM's past activities and their role in forming GJM identity. The analysis in particular draws on the group memories that activists formulate in narrative interviews, focus groups, as well as in GJM publications. In order to access activists' group memories, narrative interviews and focus groups centred on activists' oral history of the GJM overall rather than individual experiences within the GJM or biographical narratives (see e.g., della Porta, 1992). While individually retold, activists' narratives in the interviews do allow some insights into collective memories of the GJM as activists' individual stories are embedded in collective patterns of interpreting the past and hence to some extent reflect them. Furthermore, the focus groups offer additional insights into the collective and interactive dimensions of narratives and allow a triangulation of narrative patterns.

A total of seventy-one narrative interviews and three focus groups were conducted with GJM activists in Italy, Germany and Poland in 2011, 2012 and 2015 (see details in appendix A). In addition, fifteen expert interviews were conducted with academics and journalists familiar with the GJM in their respective country. The large majority of interviews were conducted between spring 2011 and spring 2012 with twenty to twenty-six activist interviews per country. In each country, in addition, four to six expert interviews and one focus group were conducted. All of the activists interviewed were centrally involved in the GJM but differ with respect to their gender, age (20–70 years old in 2001) and regional origin as well as with respect to their role within the GJM (central organisers as well as more 'rank-and-file' activists) and their feeling of belongingness.

Furthermore, the interviewed activists have different sectorial affiliations. The GJM brought together activists not only from different countries but also from different political traditions. To take into account this diversity, interviewees differ in their ideological backgrounds, action repertoires and thematic focus. More specifically, I distinguish between three sectors within each country, drawing on existing research about the European GJM (in particular Andretta et al., 2003; della Porta et al., 2006): an anti-neoliberal sector, an eco-pacifist sector and an anti-capitalist sector. The anti-neoliberal sector is composed mainly of reformist groups that aim to control the market through politics; it includes trade unions, left political parties, Attac and other NGOs. The eco-pacifist sector encompasses largely reformist environmentalist groups and organisations as well as secular and religious peace and solidarity groups. The anti-capitalist sector is composed of more radical and revolutionary groups, ranging from squatters to anarchist and Trotskyist groups, which oppose capitalist structures more fundamentally and seek radical changes instead of reform.[15] The interviews and focus groups with activists as well as the GJM publications analysed in this book are evenly distributed across these sectors (only with respect to the eco-pacifist sector in Poland, fewer interviews were conducted as this sector is very small in Poland; see the Introduction chapter).[16]

In addition to the interviews and focus groups conducted with activists in 2011 and 2012, the book's analysis includes additional data in order to trace changes in GJM identity over time: on the one hand, follow-up interviews were conducted with a small group of Italian activists in 2015 (using the same questionnaire; see details in chapter 4 and appendix A). On the other hand, I analysed central GJM publications in Italy, Germany and Poland as well as internationally between 1997 and 2005. These publications encompass individual and collective publications by GJM activists – including but not limited to activists interviewed in 2011 and 2012 – and cover the different GJM sectors (see appendix B).

Each of the book's empirical chapters draws on a particular combination of this data: chapters 2 and 3 focus on activists' narratives in the interviews and focus groups conducted in 2011 and 2012, in particular with respect to activists who feel like part of the GJM at large. Chapter 4 compares activists' narratives across time and across different degrees of belongingness drawing on three sources of data: first, a part of the interviews from 2011 and 2012 (activists who no longer or do not primarily consider themselves part of the GJM); second, on follow-up interviews conducted in 2015; and third, on selected GJM publications between 1997 and 2005.

NOTES

1. This is a view widely shared among social movement scholars; see, for example, della Porta & Diani (2006), Snow & McAdam (2000), and Rucht (2008); see also Calhoun (1993) and Castells (2001).

2. For an overview of the literature, see Polletta & Jasper (2001), Hunt & Benford (2008), Flesher Fominaya (2010a), Daphi (2011), Haunss (2004), Snow & McAdam (2000) and Jasper et al. (2015).

3. I use the term *meaning making* in the following to refer to this social construction of meaning, which in addition to cognitive evaluations includes emotional and moral judgements (Kurzman, 2008).

4. Various movement scholars locate collective identity at the individual level rather than the collective level, for example as an 'individual's cognitive, moral and emotional connection with a broader community, category, practice, or institution' (Polletta & Jasper, 2001, p. 285). Drawing on social psychology, collective identity in these cases is understood as part of or enlargement of a person's individual self-concept, fulfilling certain individual functions such as belongingness, distinctiveness, respect, understanding and agency (e.g., Klandermans, 2001; Simon & Klandermans, 2001; McCright & Dunlap, 2015).

5. Taylor & Whittier's distinction between consciousness, boundaries and negotiation was employed, for example, by Wall (2005), Hunt & Benford (2008) and Choup (2008).

6. While also constituting a way of knowing, social boundaries differ from shared cognitions as they concern knowledge about the surrounding social relations rather than a more general analysis of the world and its problems. But social boundaries may of course draw on shared cognitions (e.g., diagnostic and prognostic frames) to distinguish one's own group from that of 'the others'.

7. This book hence disagrees with the argument put forward by some movement scholars (e.g., Bennett & Segerberg, 2012; McDonald, 2002) that collective identity

overall loses its centrality in the context of heterogeneous and (digitally) networked movements. While closed and comprehensive movement identities may indeed be less relevant in these cases, overall collective identity does not lose its significance for movement dynamics here, but continues to shape collective action, however open and fluid it may be (see also Flesher Fominaya, 2010a; Gerbaudo & Treré, 2015).

8. Both studies are based on a combination of movement materials (mainly calls for action) and questionnaires with participants at transnational meetings of the GJM. While Andretta et al. (2003) focus on the transnational protests in Genoa (Italy) in 2001, della Porta et al. (2006) extend this by including data on the European Social Forum in Florence (Italy) in 2002 (movement materials and questionnaires) and the World Social Forums in Porto Alegre (Brazil) in 2001 and 2002 (movement materials).

9. Like other scholarly works (e.g., Polletta 1998b, 2006; Davis, 2002), this book uses the terms *narrative* and *story* interchangeably to avoid confusion. Scholars have drawn various distinctions between stories and narratives that differ considerably (see also Polletta et al., 2011). For example some scholars define 'story' as the 'what' of a narrative, the events recounted, in contrast to the 'how' of a narrative, that is, the overall 'narrative discourse' following the work of Seymour Chatman (1986), while others define 'stories' as single accounts in contrast to shared collective narratives (see e.g., Prins et al., 2013).

10. The term *plot* here is used differently than in common English usage: it does not refer to a certain type of story; rather, it refers to the structuring principle that holds a story together – the logical and causal structure in which events occur (Ricoeur, 1984; Todorov & Weinstein, 1969).

11. With such a narrative approach, representations of social relations and actions are analysed rather than exploring the interactions directly. In this vein, emotions during protest events are studied only indirectly, in contrast to the studies following an enactment approach.

12. For an overview of the literature on collective memory, see Harris et al. (2008).

13. For a useful overview, see, for example, Abbott (2008).

14. Such an approach to the narrative formation of identity is also frequently employed beyond social movements; see, for example, Polletta et al. (2013) for narratives about rape, Prins et al. (2013) on Moroccan-Dutch youth or Rappaport (2000) on community building.

15. Arguably this distinction fits better in some cases than in others. In particular, in Poland the eco-pacifist sector is very small as Catholic groups and human rights and international aid associations were not involved in the GJM (see the Introduction chapter and chapter 2). Furthermore, in Germany, the eco-pacifist sector included both reformist solidarity groups as well as more radical ones (see the Introduction chapter and Brand, 2005). However, this distinction was chosen as it best covers the GJM's different strands within all three case studies.

16. Six to ten activists were interviewed per national sector (with the exception of the Polish eco-pacifist sector). Focus groups included activists from each sector (at least one, see appendix A).

Chapter 2

Differences in Narrating the GJM

Where and when did this movement of movements originate? Some say it began on November 30, 1999, as the World Trade Organisation (WTO) tried to meet in a city reeking of tear gas and was paralysed by tens of thousands of demonstrators. Others think it started on New Year's Day, 1994, when the North American Free Trade Agreement (NAFTA) came into effect and the Zapatistas emerged from the mountain mist of south-eastern Mexico, declaring war on the Mexican army and neoliberalism. (Doc9-INT, para. 3)

Observers have often identified the 'Battle of Seattle' as the Global Justice Movement's (GJM) founding moment. However, as the quote above illustrates, opinions about the movement's starting point diverge among GJM activists. Perspectives on the GJM's central events and actors differ depending on whose GJM story one looks at, as this first empirical chapter will show. In particular, I will explore country- and sector-specific patterns in how activists remember the GJM in 2011 and 2012. As I will show, activists' narratives significantly differ between Italy, Germany and Poland with respect to the events and actors that they consider central. In addition to national differences, I also find sector-specific patterns in activists' narratives that are similar across the three countries.

Below I will first explore the differences in how activists in Italy, Germany and Poland recount the GJM. I will show how narratives differ between the three countries as activists focus primarily on national GJM developments and hence consider different constellations of actors and events relevant. Furthermore, activists' narratives also differ between countries since they reveal different degrees of congruence: activists agree on central actors, events and success to a larger extent in some cases (especially in Italy) and less in others (especially in Poland).

In the second part, I will shed light on sector-specific patterns that activists' narratives share across the three countries. I will show how activists from the anti-neoliberal, the eco-pacifist and the anti-capitalist sectors focus on different actors and events. Actors and events closest to the political perspective and repertoire of the respective sector are more central in the narratives. For example, events such as the World and European Social Forums are much more prominent in narratives by more moderate activists from the anti-neoliberal and eco-pacifist sectors, while activists from the anti-capitalist sector put much more emphasis on counter-summits.

The comparison below combines quantitative and qualitative elements of analysis. In this way, the chapter considers the events and actors that activists identify as central both in terms of frequency (how often are events and actors mentioned?[1]) and with respect to evaluations (what meanings do activists attribute to events and actors?) in order to cover different levels of narrative meaning making (see chapter 1).

REMEMBERING THE GJM IN ITALY

Similar to activists in Germany and Poland, Italian activists primarily focus on GJM developments in their own country as central events and actors recounted are predominantly based in Italy. In contrast to German and especially Polish activists, however, the narratives of Italian activists reveal a higher degree of congruence as activists across sectors largely agree on central actors and events as well as on the beginning and end of the GJM. Furthermore, compared to both German and Polish activists, Italian activists identify a broader spectrum of relevant GJM actors. With respect to GJM events, however, Italian narratives concentrate on very few events, in particular the counter-summit in Genoa in 2001, within a short time span between 1999 and 2004. Also, in contrast to German and Polish activists, Italian activists consider the GJM to have ended already in 2004, and they largely agree across sectors on the central reasons for this decline.

The Central Groups of the GJM in Italy

Italian activists identify a broad spectrum of groups involved in the GJM and largely agree on the role of these actors. The groups and organisations activists consider especially central strongly overlap with scholarly accounts (see the Introduction chapter) and include in particular the *Centri Sociali* and the networks linked to them (*Tute Bianche* and later *Disobbedienti*), the association ARCI (*Associazione Ricreativa e Culturale Italiana*), Catholic peace and

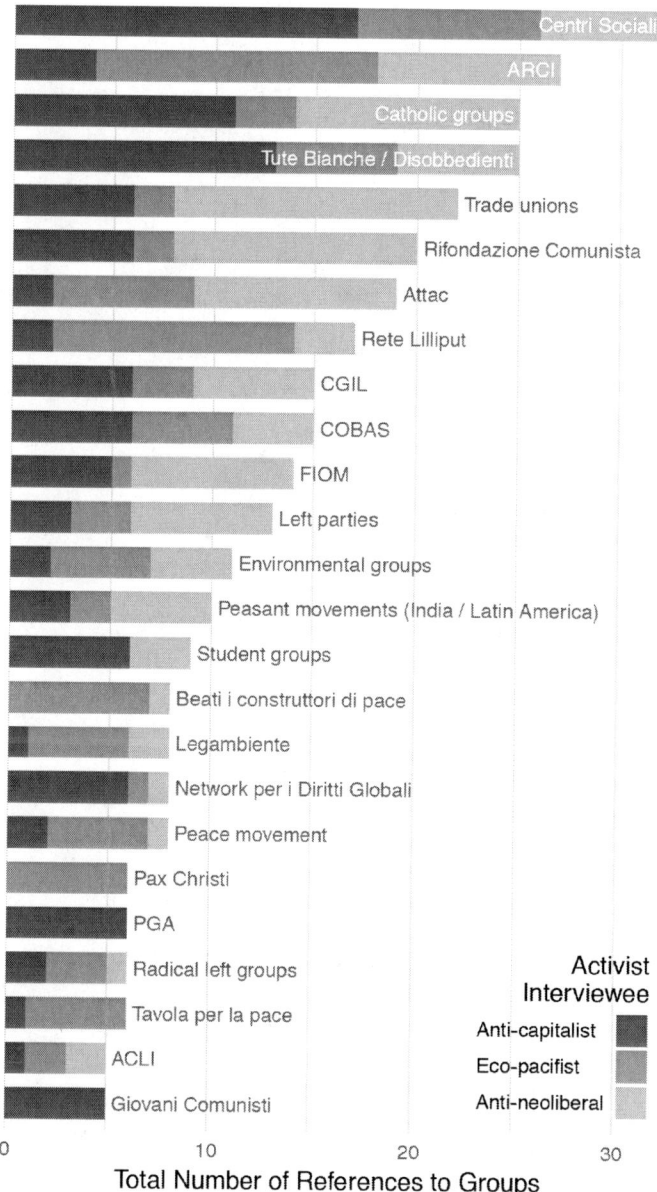

Figure 2.1   Frequency of GJM Groups in Italian Narratives. The figure only includes groups which activists mentioned five times and more. References to groups are relatively evenly distributed (references ≥3 at least two activists, ≥6 at least 3 activists, ≥10 at least 4 activists, ≥20 at least 6 activists, ≥30 at least 9 activists; ≥40 at least 11 activists).

solidarity groups, grassroots trade unions and the party *Partito della Rifondazione Comunista* (PRC) (see Figure 2.1).

With respect to groups within the anti-capitalist sector, activists across sectors clearly identify the *Centri Sociali* and the networks linked to them as major GJM actors. Not only are the *Centri Sociali* together with the *Tute Bianche* and the *Disobbedienti* the actors most frequently mentioned in activists' narratives overall (see Figure 2.1). Activists across sectors also identify them unanimously as central actors in GJM mobilisations, despite the fact that a number of more moderate activists, especially from the eco-pacifist sector, point out their frustration about some of their activities, in particular their clashes with the police.

Within the anti-neoliberal sector, trade unions and the communist party PRC are most frequently mentioned by all activists (see Figure 2.1). Indeed, Italian activists across sectors consider trade unions to have played a central role in the Italian GJM, and they are aware of the fact that this relationship was different in other European countries (in particular, France and Germany; for details see Daphi, 2014). However, not all unions are regarded as central actors of the GJM. Across all sectors, activists describe radical and grassroots unions to be central, in particular the unions of COBAS (*Confederazione dei Comitati di Base*) and the metal workers union FIOM (*Federazione Impiegati Operai Metallurgici*). However, the more established trade union confederations CGIL (*Confederazione Generale Italiana del Lavoro*) and especially the Catholic CISL (*Confederazione Italiana Sindacati Lavoratori*) as well as the UIL (*Unione Italiana del Lavoro*) are thought to be more marginal, in particular by eco-pacifist and anti-capitalist activists. Activists explain that their marginality is largely due to the fact that these unions decided not to participate in the counter-summit in Genoa and in some cases even discouraged participation in the event (in particular the CISL). Only anti-neoliberal activists consider the CGIL as a central actor in the GJM.

While political parties overall are rarely mentioned, references to the communist party PRC are prominent in activists' narratives (see Figure 2.1). The party is seen as a central part of the GJM across all sectors, with only a few exceptions among eco-pacifist activists who consider PRC more marginal. Finally, the Italian chapter of *Attac*, while relatively often mentioned (see Figure 2.1), is regarded as a central actor in the early years only by anti-neoliberal and eco-pacifist activists; anti-capitalist activists perceive it to be overall more marginal.

With respect to the eco-pacifist sector, Catholic groups and the association ARCI are most frequently mentioned (see Figure 2.1). While ARCI is much more prominent in narratives by anti-neoliberal and especially eco-pacifist activists (see Figure 2.1), activists from all sectors, also the more radical activists, define this organisation as a central part of the GJM in Italy. Also

Catholic groups are held to be central actors of the GJM across all sectors, in particular those linked to *Rete Lilliput*, a network of Catholic and secular peace and solidarity groups (see the Introduction chapter). However, only eco-pacifist activists hold more established Catholic organisations such as *Pax Christi* and *Caritas* to be part of the GJM (see the section "Sectorial Differences across Countries"). Similarly, environmental groups such as *Legambiente*, while mentioned across all sectors (see Figure 2.1), are thought to be central GJM actors only by eco-pacifist and anti-neoliberal activists. Anti-capitalist activists hardly mention environmental groups or clearly define them as marginal – either because they are considered too institutional (especially the environmental NGO *Legambiente*) or because they are perceived to be part of a different (environmental) movement.

The Central Events of the GJM in Italy

More than their Polish and especially German counterparts, Italian activists focus their narratives on a small selection of events and in particular on the counter-summit in Genoa in 2001. Also the time span of GJM activities that activists identify overall is shorter, starting in 1999 with the protests against the war in Kosovo and the counter-summit in Seattle in 1999 and ending

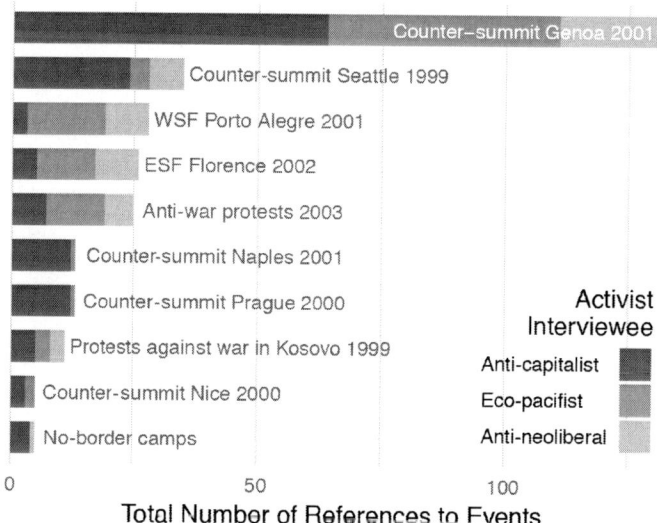

Figure 2.2 Frequency of GJM Events in Italian Narratives. The figure only includes events which activists mentioned five times and more, and which they consider to form part of the GJM's cycle of mobilisation. References to events are relatively evenly distributed (references ≥3 at least two activists, ≥6 at least 3 activists, ≥10 at least 4 activists, ≥20 at least 6 activists, ≥30 at least 9 activists; ≥40 at least 11 activists).

around 2004 after the demonstrations against the war in Iraq in 2003. Activists' focus on these events means that some GJM mobilisations tend to be neglected in activists' narratives, in particular early ones such as the protests against the G7 in Naples in 1994 and later ones such as the prospering local social forums across Italy from 2003 onwards (see the Introduction chapter).

While not the largest event in terms of participation, the counter-summit in Genoa in 2001 is by far the most prominent event in activists' narratives, mentioned more than four times as often as other events (see Figure 2.2). Other events that activists frequently refer to – while much less than to the counter-summit in Genoa – are the counter-summit in Seattle in 1999, the first World Social Forum (WSF) in Porto Alegre (Brazil) in 2001, the first European Social Forum (ESF) in Florence and the demonstrations against the war in Iraq in 2003 (see Figure 2.2).

Across sectors, activists define the counter-summit in Genoa as *the* crucial GJM event, despite other protest events in Italy being larger, in particular the anti-war demonstrations in 2003 and the ESF in Florence in 2002 (see the Introduction chapter). The event in Genoa is regarded as a watershed moment in the sense of demonstrating the strength of the GJM in building broad coalitions and paving the way for further mobilisations against neoliberal globalisation, while also triggering later splits (see chapter 3). Emblematic of the centrality of this event is also that activists often determine which (other) groups form part of the GJM with respect to their role during the counter-summit in Genoa (Daphi, 2017).

Next to the counter-summit in Genoa, activists across sectors in particular regard the ESF in Florence and the anti-war demonstrations as peak events of the GJM. Within this peak phase, anti-neoliberal and eco-pacifist activists tend to stress the anti-war demonstrations more, while activists from the anti-capitalist sector rather emphasise the role of the counter-summit in Genoa and other counter-summits and consider especially the first WSF in Porto Alegre more marginal (see the section 'Sectorial Differences across Countries').

In contrast to the peak events, activists across all sectors define the counter-summit in Seattle and the demonstrations against the war in Kosovo in 1999 as crucial first steps in mobilising globally as they strengthened transnational exchanges between activists (especially the counter-summit in Seattle) as well as a transnational analysis of problems (see also chapter 3). In addition, Italian activists stress Seattle's role in addressing the deficit of democratic legitimacy of international organisations.

Across sectors, activists consider the GJM to have ended around 2004. Mobilisations after 2004 hence are largely neglected in Italian narratives, such as the counter-summit in Heiligendamm in 2007 and the WSFs after 2003. After 2004, the GJM is described to have notably declined, with activities becoming more local and issue specific (see also Zamponi & Daphi,

2014). Compared to activists in Germany and Poland, Italian activists identify this end and its causes more clearly and coherently. Activists delineate three reasons for the GJM's decline after 2004, which are largely linked to a notion of defeat. First, the failure of the anti-war demonstrations in 2003 discouraged further mobilisation. Activists highlight how the demonstrations' incapacity to stop the Italian support of the war in Iraq, despite a very high number of participants, crucially frustrated activists and led to divisions. Second, activists stress that the formation of a centre-left coalition from 2004 onwards (getting into government in 2006 with Romano Prodi as prime minister) created a considerable divide between moderate and radical left groups since central GJM organisations such as the communist party PRC and ARCI participated in or endorsed the new left government (see also Daphi, 2013; Zamponi & Daphi, 2014). Third, the repression experienced during the protests in Genoa in 2001 and the following counter-summits is held to have weakened the GJM, revealing the limits of this kind of mobilisation and creating divides about tactics. Activists often describe the events in Genoa as a personal and political trauma that was difficult to recover from and that somewhat immobilised the movement in Italy.

While these three factors are shared across sectors, anti-capitalist activists tend to stress the role of repression in the context of the counter-summit in Genoa more and hence tend to identify an earlier decline of the GJM, while anti-neoliberal activists in turn tend to put more emphasis on the divisions that the Prodi government created (see the section 'Sectorial Differences across Countries').

Though considered a new phase of mobilisation, activists identify continuities with respect to certain elements of the GJM in mobilisations after 2004, in particular regarding addressed issues. Activists across sectors especially stress the continuation of the GJM's opposition to neoliberal policies of privatisation and its emphasis on common goods in the Italian campaign against the privatisation of water in 2011. Activists from the eco-pacifist sector additionally stress the continued concern with environmental issues in this campaign. Furthermore, a number of activists from the anti-neoliberal and anti-capitalist sectors see continuities between the GJM and European protests against austerity with respect to addressing the issues of social justice and democratic rule as well as regarding horizontal forms of organisation (see also Zamponi & Daphi, 2014).[2]

REMEMBERING THE GJM IN GERMANY

Like the activists interviewed in Italy and Poland, German activists focus their narratives on GJM developments in Germany since the central events and actors recounted are predominantly based in this country. Compared to Italian activists, narratives by German activists are less congruent, especially since German activists disagree more on central actors as well as reasons of the GJM's decline. Furthermore, in contrast to both Italian and Polish activists, German activists concentrate their narratives on a few actors, in particular the German chapter of *Attac*. With respect to GJM events, German activists identify a broader range of relevant events than activists in Italy as well as a longer duration of the GJM from 1998 to 2007. German activists are less explicit and consistent about the causes of the GJM's decline than activists in Italy. Also, in contrast to activists in both Italy and Poland, a part of the German activists associate the end of the GJM with successes rather than failures.

The Central Groups of the GJM in Germany

German activists concentrate their narratives on few actors, in particular the German chapter of *Attac*, with the tendency to overlook the broader variety of groups involved in the GJM in Germany (see the Introduction chapter). Besides *Attac*, activists across sectors consider the post-autonomist network *Interventionistische Linke* (IL) and environmental groups as central groups of the GJM. Beyond these groups, however, activists' opinions about the central actors of the GJM partly diverge across the sectors.

With respect to actors from the anti-neoliberal sector, NGOs are very prominent in activists' narratives, corresponding with the overall central role of NGOs in the German GJM (see the Introduction chapter). This elevated status of NGOs is mainly due to the central role of *Attac* in activists' narratives. *Attac* is mentioned more than twice as often as most other groups (see Figure 2.3) and is considered a very central actor of the GJM in Germany across all sectors. This is not surprising because *Attac* worked as a network that brought together various groups involved in the GJM in Germany (see the Introduction chapter). Not all activists evaluate this central role of *Attac* positively though; especially actors from the anti-capitalist sector regard *Attac* as too dominant following the counter-summit in Genoa in 2001. Another NGO which activists across sectors describe as a central actor and which they frequently mention (see Figure 2.3) is in particular *World Economy, Ecology and Development* (WEED) – an NGO closely connected with *Attac*.

Contrary to Italy as well as Poland, activists in Germany consider trade unions more marginal GJM actors – with reference to low links between social movements and unions in Germany more generally (see the Introduction chapter). While activists often mention trade unions (see Figure 2.3), only certain unions are thought to be part of the GJM, especially the metal workers' union IG-Metall and the union Ver.di, which participated mainly in later GJM mobilisations on social policies in Germany (see the Introduction

Figure 2.3   Frequency of GJM Groups in German Narratives. The figure only includes groups which activists mentioned five times and more. References to groups are relatively evenly distributed (references ≥3 at least two activists, ≥6 at least 3 activists, ≥10 at least 4 activists, ≥20 at least 6 activists, ≥30 at least 9 activists; ≥40 at least 11 activists).

chapter). More than Italian activists, opinions among German activists diverge on how central even these unions are. In particular, activists from the eco-pacifist sector consider them more marginal due to the unions' overall lack of attention to environmental issues. In addition, anti-capitalist activists only partly describe Ver.di and IG-Metall as actors of the GJM at all; in particular, (post-)autonomist activists do not mention them at all or identify only small or radical unions from the Global South as part of the GJM.

Also left political parties play a marginal role in German activists' narratives. Activists across sectors do mention the left party *Die Linke* and the green party *Bündnis 90/die Grünen*; however, both are considered either marginal (especially by anti-neoliberal activists) or not part of the GJM. More than the parties as such, the political foundations linked to *Die Linke* and the green party (*Rosa-Luxemburg-Stiftung Stiftung* and *Heinrich-Böll-Stiftung*, respectively) and especially the youth organisations linked to each (*Linksjugend* and *Grüne Jugend*, respectively) are thought to be parts of the GJM – at least by activists from the anti-neoliberal sector.

With respect to actors from the eco-pacifist sector, activists from all sectors hold environmental groups and NGOs to be central GJM actors across sectors, especially the German chapter of *Greenpeace* and the environmental NGO BUND (*Bund für Umwelt und Naturschutz Deutschland*). Hence, German activists in contrast to their Italian and Polish counterparts stress the central role of environmental groups in the GJM. In this vein, the issue of environmental injustice and destruction is also much more prominent in German narratives. Faith-based and peace groups – while frequently mentioned (see Figure 2.3) – are considered marginal beyond activists from the eco-pacifist sector, especially by activists from the anti-capitalist sector. Activists from the anti-capitalist sector regard particularly large and established Christian charity NGOs such as *Brot für die Welt* and the German chapter of *Pax Christi* to be peripheral.

Regarding groups from the anti-capitalist sector, activists most frequently mention the post-autonomist network IL (see Figure 2.3). Activists across all sectors consider the IL a central actor of the GJM, though it came into being only relatively late, namely in the lead-up to the counter-summit in Heiligendamm in 2007 (see the Introduction chapter). In contrast, anti-capitalist activists connected to grassroots networks such as the PGA (*Peoples' Global Action*) are seen as having a much less central role, as is the German internationalist grassroots network BUKO (*Bundeskoordination Internationalismus*) (see also Figure 2.3), although they were very active, particularly in the early phase of the German GJM (see the Introduction chapter). Only anti-capitalist activists describe PGA as a central part of the GJM (see the section 'Sectorial Differences across Countries'), while BUKO is regarded as part of the GJM by both anti-capitalist and eco-pacifist groups due to its strong focus on issues of international solidarity. Anti-fascist groups such as the *Antifa* as well as Trotskyist groups such as *Linksruck* are defined as part of the GJM only by some, namely anti-capitalist activists.

The Central Events of the GJM in Germany

Compared to both the Italian and Polish activists, German activists regard a broader range of events to form part of the GJM and include more GJM events abroad. The main phase of the GJM is identified to be longer, starting in 1998 with the anti-MAI campaign to 2007 with the counter-summit in Heiligendamm.

Activists mention the counter-summits in Heiligendamm in 2007, in Genoa in 2001 and in Seattle in 1999 most frequently (see Figure 2.4) and consider them the most central events of the GJM. The counter-summit in Heiligendamm is defined as the key event in the German GJM as it successfully mobilised a broad range of groups in joint activities, despite its

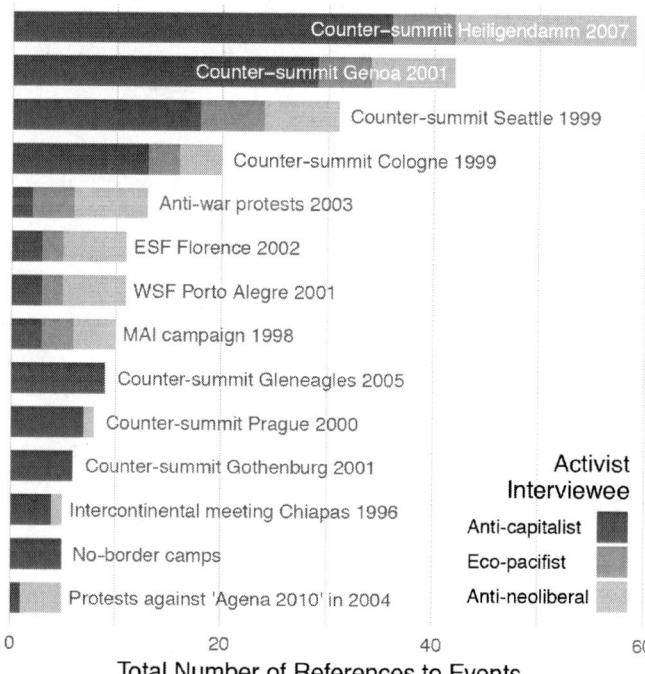

Figure 2.4 Frequency of GJM Events in German Narratives. The figure only includes events which activists mentioned five times and more, and which they consider to form part of the GJM's cycle of mobilisation. References to events are relatively evenly distributed (references ≥3 at least two activists, ≥6 at least 3 activists, ≥10 at least 4 activists, ≥20 at least 6 activists, ≥30 at least 9 activists; ≥40 at least 11 activists).

occurrence after a period of low mobilisation in Germany and its inclusion of several new groups and networks (see the Introduction chapter). Activists identify the counter-summits in Seattle and Genoa as international culmination points of the GJM, points of departure that provided central impulses for further mobilisation against neoliberal globalisation. The counter-summit in Seattle is especially seen to have kicked off new kinds of cross-sectorial cooperation, despite the low participation in and attention to the event by German activists (see the Introduction chapter). Activists describe the counter-summit in Genoa in particular to have brought the global movement to Europe (see chapter 3). While bringing as many as 500,000 people to the streets (see the Introduction chapter), activists consider the demonstrations against the war in Iraq in 2003 and the subsequent years less as central GJM events; activists from the anti-capitalist and anti-neoliberal sectors in fact tend to think of these demonstrations rather as another movement (the international peace movement) to which the GJM contributed. Furthermore, the first WSF in Brazil in 2001 and the ESF in Florence in 2002 are regarded as central GJM events only by anti-neoliberal and eco-pacifist activists (see the section 'Sectorial Differences across Countries').

Activists across all sectors define the anti-MAI campaign in 1998 and the counter-summit in Cologne in 1999 as central events in preparing the GJM's peak phase. These events are seen to have primarily facilitated the building of transnational activists' networks around the issue of global justice. Across all sectors, activists additionally identify the protests against the meeting of the IMF and World Bank in 1988 in Berlin as other important precursors of the GJM, while not forming part of the GJM. Activists describe how these protests brought together for the first time different groups around the issue of global finance such as environmental organisations, international solidarity groups and trade unions.

Activists across all sectors consider the GJM to have ended after the counter-summit in Heiligendamm in 2007. Similar to the Italian activists, German activists perceive subsequent mobilisations as more local and issue specific since they lost the GJM's capacity to stimulate a broad mobilisation; sectorial and transnational links could not be maintained and the general thematic focus shifted to specific issues such as migration or social security. Compared to activists in Italy, German activists identify the causes of this decline less clearly and coherently. While the decline is considered to immediately follow the counter-summit in Heiligendamm in 2007, it is hardly interpreted to be due to a failure of this protest, in contrast to the central role Italian activists attribute to the failure of the anti-war demonstrations. German activists, in fact, largely interpret the counter-summit in Heiligendamm as a success rather than a failure (see also chapter 3). A number of activists do mention disputes about protest tactics during the counter-summit in Heiligendamm,[3] but only very few identify them as reasons for the GJM's decline. German activists instead more generally describe how after the counter-summit in Heiligendamm the broad mobilisation for issues of global justice lost momentum. This is attributed either to activists' general fatigue or to the need for new alliances and forms of mobilisation in the context of the financial crisis. Furthermore, a number of activists stress how mobilisations became more difficult as the claims of the GJM became more mainstream and were increasingly picked up by institutional politics, for example, the tax on financial transactions (Tobin tax). While activists from the anti-neoliberal and eco-pacifist sectors perceive this development more positively, in terms of the GJM's success in raising public awareness about the injustices created by neoliberal globalisation, anti-capitalist activists describe this development more negatively as a process of co-optation and increasing repression (see the section 'Sectorial Differences across Countries').

Similar to Italian activists, German activists identify continuities of the GJM in later mobilisations with respect to addressed issues. Especially the Occupy and Indignados movements are understood to continue the GJM's concern with questions of social justice and political participation. Activists across sectors, however, consider the tactics of the anti-austerity protests as more radical due to the focus on occupations. A number of eco-pacifist and anti-capitalist activists in addition highlight the continued concern with environmental justice, for example, in the context of protests against the UN Climate Change conference in Copenhagen in 2009.

REMEMBERING THE GJM IN POLAND

Polish activists' narratives have a particularly strong focus on national GJM developments. Furthermore, stories by Polish activists are less congruent than in Germany and especially in Italy since activists disagree considerably more on both central actors and events. In this vein, while Polish activists refer to a broad range of GJM actors, there is little agreement across sectors on which groups are central. With respect to GJM events, Polish activists refer to few events while identifying a relatively long GJM time frame from 1999 to 2007. Among these few events, activists agree on the centrality of only a part of them, and most of these events are based in Poland or surrounding countries. In particular, local protests related to workers' rights are more central than in the Italian and German cases. Polish activists additionally are less explicit and coherent about the timing and causes of the GJM's decline than activists in Germany and especially in Italy.

The Central Groups of the GJM in Poland

Polish activists mention a variety of groups involved in the GJM in Poland; however, in contrast to German and especially Italian activists, they agree much less on which of these groups actually form a central part of the movement. Only anarchists and anarcho-syndicalist groups as well as small feminist and environmental groups are regarded as central by all activists. Beyond this, activists do not concur in the groups they mention, or they disagree on their centrality.

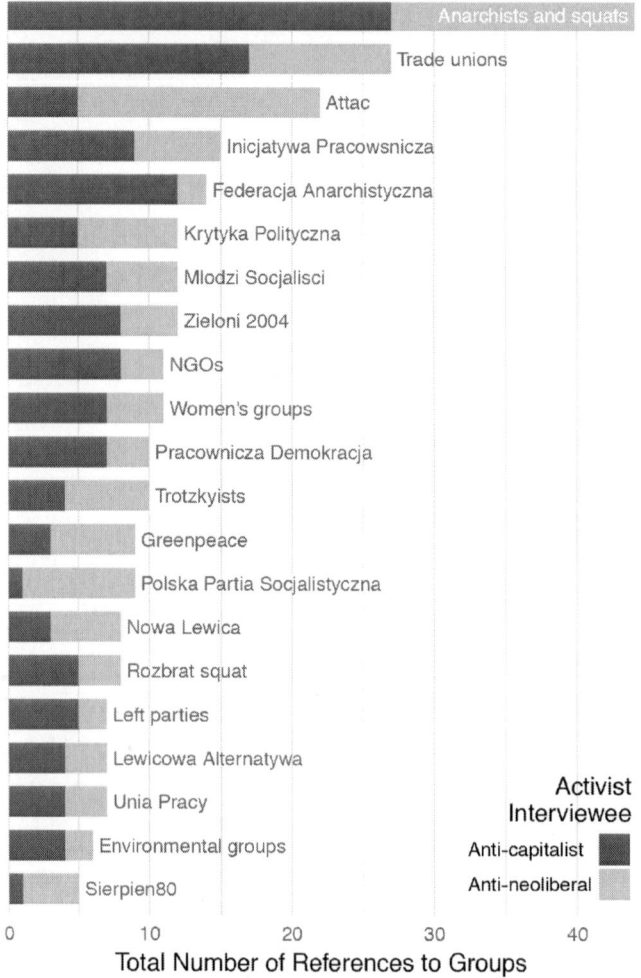

Figure 2.5   Frequency of GJM Groups in Polish Narratives. The figure only includes groups which activists mentioned five times and more. References to groups are relatively evenly distributed (references ≥3 at least two activists, ≥6 at least 3 activists, ≥10 at least 4 activists, ≥20 at least 6 activists, ≥30 at least 9 activists; ≥40 at least 11 activists).

Groups from the anti-capitalist sector are particularly prominent in all activists' narratives, especially anarchist groups. Activists most frequently mention anarchist groups in their narratives – in the form of a general reference to anarchists and squats and references to specific anarchist groups such as the national anarchist federation *Federacja Anarchistyczna* (see Figure 2.5). Besides being frequently mentioned, activists across all sectors agree that anarchists formed a central part of the GJM in Poland. In addition, a number of smaller socialist and Trotskyist groups are often named (see Figure 2.5) and are largely considered part of the GJM by anti-neoliberal and anti-capitalist activists (but not all mention them), in particular the Trotskyist group *Pracownicza Demokracja* and also the socialist group *Lewicowa Alternatywa*, although mentioned less often (see Figure 2.5).

With respect to groups from the anti-neoliberal sector, activists refer most frequently to trade unions and the Polish chapter of *Attac* (see Figure 2.5). While most activists believe *Attac* to be part of the GJM in Poland, they largely consider it marginal because it soon lost its strength owing to internal divisions, shrinking it to a handful of people (compare the Introduction chapter). While anti-neoliberal activists tend to regard the foundation of *Attac Poland* in 2001 as a temporary success in bringing together different groups, anti-capitalist activists in contrast tend to describe *Attac* more negatively as a failed attempt to build coalitions, if they mention it at all. Likewise, the more moderate publishing project and think tank *Krytyka Polityczna* is considered a central GJM group by the majority of anti-neoliberal activists but thought to be more marginal by anti-capitalist activists.

While frequently mentioned (see Figure 2.5), trade unions are largely not defined as part of the GJM across sectors, especially larger union confederations such as OPZZ (*Ogólnopolskie Porozumienie Związków Zawodowych*) and the more conservative *Solidarność* union. Across sectors, activists consider only smaller and radical trade unions a part of the GJM, in particular the anarcho-syndicalist group *Inicjatywa Pracownicza*. Only a number of anti-neoliberal activists regard as central to the GJM the small but more established union *Sierpien80* (August80), linked to the labour party *Polska Partia Pracy* (PPP) as well as *Konfederacja Pracy*, a union forming part of the trade union confederation OPZZ.

Similarly, activists rarely perceive parties as part of the GJM. In fact, only the socialist group *Młodzi Socjaliści*, a split from the left party *Unia Pracy*, is understood as a part of the GJM by both anti-neoliberal and anti-capitalist activists, though founded only in 2005 (see the Introduction chapter). Conversely, the Polish socialist party *Polska Partia Socjalistyczna*, although mentioned in almost ten instances (see Figure 2.5), is not thought to be part of the GJM. And only anti-neoliberal activists describe the small labour party PPP as well as the left party *Nowa Lewica* and the green party *Zieloni 2004* as part of the GJM (more or less central). The small left party *Unia Pracy* is considered a part of the movement by a number of anti-capitalist activists, especially those affiliated with socialist and communist groups.

Eco-pacifist groups are very marginal in activists' narratives, in particular faith-based groups and large aid NGOs, corresponding to their overall low involvement in the Polish GJM (see the Introduction chapter). While activists across all sectors mention NGOs in about ten instances (see Figure 2.5), they exclude most of them explicitly from the movement (see also Daphi, 2014b), especially in the sense of human rights NGOs (such as the Polish chapter of *Amnesty International* or *the Helsinki Foundation for Human Rights*). Activists consider only smaller feminist and environmental NGOs and groups as central actors of the GJM (see also Figure 2.5). Large environmental NGOs such as *Greenpeace*, on the other hand, are often identified as marginal, especially by anti-capitalist activists.

The Central Events of the GJM in Poland

Polish activists' narratives concentrate on few events within a time frame as long as in the German case, namely from 1999, with the counter-summit in Seattle, until 2008. Overall, agreement on the role of events is notably lower than in Italy and in Germany (see the section 'Sectorial Differences across Countries'), and activists in Poland tend to be more sceptical about the overall impact of the GJM against the background of the continuing weakness of Polish civil society overall. Furthermore, the events Polish activists regard as central are largely based in Poland and address more local issues, in particular issues of workers' rights – despite Polish activists' considerable participation in international GJM events such as ESFs and various counter-summits (see the Introduction chapter).

The three most frequently mentioned events in activists' narratives are the counter-summit in Warsaw in 2004, the protests against the war in Iraq in 2003 (in Poland) and the counter-summit in Prague in 2000 (see Figure 2.6). Activists define the counter-summit in Warsaw and the anti-war protests as central GJM events in terms of their successes in mobilising a particularly large amount of people and uniting a broad range of activists as well as in challenging neoliberal thinking (see chapter 3). Anti-capitalist activists in this context stress especially the counter-summit in Warsaw and anti-neoliberal activists especially the anti-war demonstrations (see the section 'Sectorial Differences across Countries'). In addition, activists across sectors identify the counter-summit in Prague in 2000 as a central first event preparing the later peaks of the Warsaw summit in 2004 and the anti-war protests in 2003. The events in Prague in this way are described as a central impulse in

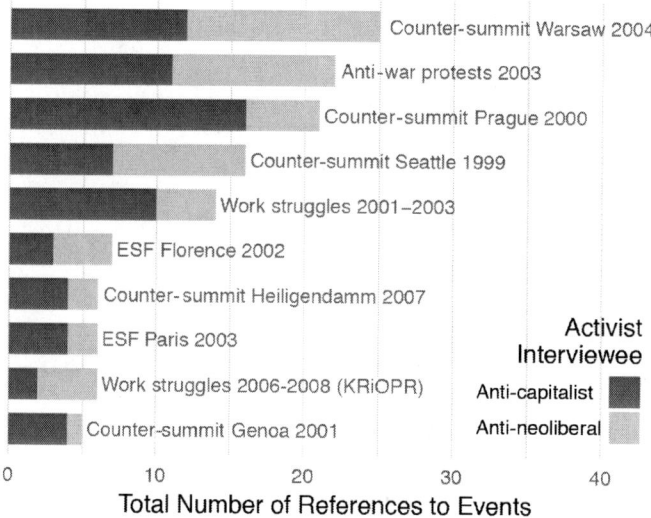

Figure 2.6 Frequency of GJM Events in Polish Narratives. The figure only includes events which activists mentioned five times and more, and which they consider to form part of the GJM's cycle of mobilisation. References to events are relatively evenly distributed (references ≥3 at least two activists, ≥6 at least 3 activists, ≥10 at least 4 activists, ≥20 at least 6 activists, ≥30 at least 9 activists; ≥40 at least 11 activists).

bringing the issue of anti-neoliberalism closer to Poland with activists starting to feel part of a larger movement and building international ties.

Beyond the counter-summit in Prague, GJM events occurring abroad, such as the counter-summits in Seattle and Genoa or the ESFs and WSFs, play a more marginal role in Polish narratives than in their Italian and German counterparts, in particular among anti-neoliberal activists. This marginality also concerns the ESFs, despite the fact that Polish activists were considerably involved in them (see the Introduction chapter). Overall, activists mention GJM events abroad much less frequently in Polish narratives (see Figure 2.6), in particular in comparison with activists in Germany. And if mentioned – such as the counter-summits in Seattle, Genoa and Heiligendamm (see Figure 2.6) – they are rarely described as incisive events. Activists rather emphasise these events' misrepresentation in Polish media (see chapter 3). Only anti-capitalist activists tend to stress these events' positive impact more, in particular with respect to the impression the counter-summit in Prague had on Polish activists (see the section 'Sectorial Differences across Countries').

Conversely, Polish activists consider various local labour struggles to form a major part of the GJM. Struggles for better working conditions are defined as a central element in the resistance against neoliberal transformation.

Accordingly, the issue of justice is framed more in relation to issues in Poland, in particular the social injustices caused by neoliberal policies introduced in Poland after 1989 and less with respect to global injustices. Activists in this context stress strikes and protests between 2001 and 2003 as highly significant, especially the large May Day demonstrations in 2001 and the strike at the cable factory in Ożarów in 2002 (see Figure 2.6). Activists describe these events as crucial first successes in bringing different left groups together and mobilising against neoliberal policies – while not yet as broad as later mobilisations (see also chapter 3).

In Poland, the GJM is considered to have ended in 2007/2008 in the context of the financial crisis and the new conditions for mobilisation it created. Similar to activists in Italy and Germany, Polish activists stress that mobilisations after 2008 had a more sector-specific and local focus than those of the GJM (see also chapter 3). However, the causes as well as the events of the GJM's decline are less clearly and coherently defined than in Italy as well as Germany. Apart from the financial crisis, activists hardly identify explicit reasons for the GJM's decline. If reasons for the decline are mentioned, they are sector specific, with anti-capitalist activists stressing divides following the counter-summit in Warsaw and anti-neoliberal activists stressing the decline of the ESFs after 2004 and splits within *Attac Poland* after 2003 (see the section 'Sectorial Differences across Countries'). Furthermore, opinions about the GJM's last mobilisations diverge across sectors. While most activists regard the counter-summit in Heiligendamm to still form part of the GJM, opinions about mobilisations after 2007 differ: A number of anti-neoliberal activists consider the work struggles related to the network KRiOPR between 2006 and 2008 (see the Introduction chapter) as part of the GJM (see also Figure 2.6), while the few anti-capitalist activists who mention these protests do not share this view and criticise how the labour party PPP exploited the protests for electoral purposes through its close ties to the involved trade union *Sierpien80*. In addition, only anti-capitalist activists describe the protests against the UN Climate Change Conference in Poznań in 2008 to form part of the GJM in Poland.

Similar to Italian and German activists, Polish activists identify continuities of certain elements of the GJM in later mobilisations, in particular with respect to addressed issues. In this vein, the various tenants' campaigns across Poland gaining momentum after the GJM's decline around 2007 (see the Introduction chapter) are seen to continue the GJM's opposition to privatisation, while their level of mobilisation is more local and specialised. Furthermore, as their Italian and German counterparts, Polish activists regard the Occupy and Indignados movements as a continuation of the GJM's concern with issues of democratic participation and especially social justice.

SECTORIAL DIFFERENCES ACROSS COUNTRIES

The three parts above show the variation in GJM narratives across countries. However, activists' narratives differ not only between countries, but also between sectors. Activists' narratives reveal sector-specific patterns that are in fact similar across the three countries. Specific events and actors are more prominent among activists from one sector rather than the other, and reasons for the movement's rise and decline differ. Differences are particularly prominent between the anti-capitalist sector, on the one hand, and the anti-neoliberal and eco-pacifist sectors, on the other. For example, counter-summits play a much more central role in anti-capitalist narratives, while World and European Social Forums and anti-war demonstrations play a more central role in anti-neoliberal and eco-pacifist narratives.

Central GJM Groups within Sectors

In activists' narratives, groups that are close to activists' own group in organisation, ideas and tactics are more prominent. In this vein, anti-neoliberal activists tend to consider other anti-neoliberal groups more central, eco-pacifist activists regard other eco-pacifist activists as central and anti-capitalist activists hold the same for anti-capitalist groups.

Narratives by *anti-capitalist activists* in Italy accordingly focus in particular on the *Centri Sociali* and the groups *Tute Bianche* and *Disobbedienti* (see Figure 2.1). In addition, anti-capitalist activists are the only ones referring to certain more radical left groups as central actors of the GJM, in particular the *Giovani Comunisti*, the youth organisation of the communist party PRC with strong connections to the *Centri Sociali*, the *Network per i Diritti Globali* and the transnational grassroots network PGA (see also Figure 2.1).

Similarly, in Germany the IL, autonomist groups and the *Antifa* are more prominent in narratives by anti-capitalist activists (see also Figure 2.3). As in Italy, anti-capitalist activists in Germany are the only ones referring to the PGA (see Figure 2.3) as a central GJM actor. Moreover, almost exclusively do German anti-capitalist activists consider the peasant movements in Latin America and India linked to *La Via Campesina* a part of the GJM (see Figure 2.3).

In Poland, anti-capitalist activists comparably consider other radical left groups more central. In particular, anarchist groups and the anarchist federation *Federacja Anarchistyczna* as well as the Trotskyists group *Pracownicza Demokracja* and the anarcho-syndicalist group *Inicjatywa Pracownicza* are more prominent in anti-capitalist narratives than in anti-neoliberal ones (see Figure 2.5). Furthermore, as described above, anti-capitalist activists tend to hold several moderate groups to be more marginal, in particular *Attac* and the trade union *Sierpien80*.

Conversely, in narratives by *anti-neoliberal activists*, moderate left groups such as *Attac* and trade unions are more central. In Italy, anti-neoliberal activists regard the traditional trade unions and especially the CGIL as more central to the GJM than other activists. And also *Attac* is considered a more crucial actor by anti-neoliberal as well as eco-pacifist activists in Italy (see also Figure 2.1). Similarly, anti-neoliberal activists in Germany most frequently refer to the trade unions Ver.di and IG-Metall (see Figure 2.3), and most clearly define them as central actors. Furthermore, only anti-neoliberal activists identify the political foundations linked to left and green parties as well as NGOs such as *Medico International* as part of the GJM. Also in Poland, *Attac* and the network KRiOPR play more central roles in narratives by anti-neoliberal activists, as does the publishing project and think tank *Krytyka Polityczna* (see also Figure 2.5). On top of that, only anti-neoliberal activists regard as part of the GJM the unions *Sierpien80* and *Konfederacja Pracy*, the left parties PPP and *Nowa Lewica* as well as the green party *Zieloni 2004* and environmental NGOs.

In narratives by activists from the *eco-pacifist sector*, environmental groups play a more central role in Italy and Germany. In Italy, especially more institutionalised environmental groups are more prominent in eco-pacifist narratives, such as the environmental NGO *Legambiente* (see Figure 2.1), and in contrast to other activists, eco-pacifist activists in Italy also consider the WWF a part of the GJM. Similarly, eco-pacifist activists in Germany pay more attention to environmental organisations than activists from other sectors (see Figure 2.3). Among Italian and German eco-pacifist activists also, faith-based groups are more central than others. In Italy, eco-pacifist activists in this vein refer most frequently to ARCI and the network *Rete Lilliput* (see Figure 2.1) and almost exclusively regard as central Catholic peace groups such as *Beati i Construttori di Pace* and *Tavolo per la pace* as well as established Catholic organisations, especially *Pax Christi*. Likewise German eco-pacifist activists are the only ones considering faith-based groups such as *Kairos Europa* and also more established Christian NGOs such as *Pax Christi* as GJM actors (see also Figure 2.3). In addition, eco-pacifist activists in these two countries tend to consider certain anti-neoliberal groups as more marginal than activists from the other two sectors: particularly the communist party PRC in Italy and the unions IG-Metall and Ver.di for Germany.

Furthermore, activists in all sectors and countries tend to refer to groups in more general terms (e.g., 'the radical left') which they do regard as part of the GJM but whom they consider less close in terms of ideology and tactics in contrast to groups perceived as similar. For example, in Italy activists from the anti-neoliberal and anti-capitalist sectors refer to Catholic groups largely in general terms instead of naming specific groups such as *Beati i construttori di pace* (see Figure 2.1). Conversely, eco-pacifist activists in Italy most frequently use the general reference 'radical left groups' (see Figure 2.1). Similarly, activists from the anti-capitalist sector in Germany tend to refer to NGOs in general terms rather than naming specific groups (with the exception of the NGO WEED; see Figure 2.3). And activists from the eco-pacifist sector in Germany tend to refer to left parties in general terms rather than naming specific parties see Figure 2.3). In Poland, activists from the anti-neoliberal sector tend to refer to anarchists in general terms rather than mentioning specific groups (such as the anarchist federation *Federacja Anarchistyczna* or the *Rozbrat* squat; see Figure 2.5). And activists from the anti-capitalist sector tend to refer to trade unions and NGOs in general terms rather than mentioning specific ones (with the exception of anarcho-syndicalist groups; see Figure 2.5).

Central GJM Events within Sectors

Next to national differences, the centrality of events significantly varies across the different movement sectors. Most strikingly, the various counter-summits are much more present in the narratives by activists from the anti-capitalist sector. Conversely, the ESFs and especially WSFs are most frequently mentioned by activists from the anti-neoliberal and eco-pacifist sectors (see Figures 2.2, 2.4 and 2.6). Furthermore, certain events are exclusively referred to by activists from a particular sector. These concern largely sector-specific meetings and mobilisations identified to have been crucial in strengthening transnational cooperation, mutual learning and the exchange of resources prior to the respective peak events (see also chapter 3).

Central Events within the Anti-capitalist Sector

In all three countries, counter-summits overall are more central in narratives by anti-capitalist activists both in the GJM's growth and in its decline. In Italy, this concerns in particular the counter-summits in Nice, in 2000; Prague, in 2000; and Naples, in 2001. These events are almost exclusively mentioned by activists from the anti-capitalist sector (see Figure 2.2). Italian anti-capitalist Italian activists also consider the counter-summit in Prague part of the GJM's peak events, in contrast to activists from the anti-neoliberal and eco-pacifist sectors. Furthermore, the counter-summit in Naples in 2001 is seen as a crucial event in the build-up towards the peak of the movement as it forged new international ties and analytical frameworks. Also the counter-summits in Seattle and in Genoa are much more prominent in narratives from anti-capitalist activists (see also Figure 2.2). These activists identify the events in Genoa more as a peak of mobilisation than the ESF in Florence and the anti-war demonstrations in 2003 (see the section 'Remembering the GJM in Italy'). On top of counter-summits, Italian anti-capitalist activists underline the role of the intensifying autonomist network across Europe in the late 1990s, particularly in the context of Zapatista meetings in Europe and no-border camps. This growing exchange is perceived to have been crucial in preparing the GJM's peak events since it strengthened international and horizontal forms of organisation (see also chapter 3).

Similarly, among German anti-capitalist activists, counter-summits are very central. The counter-summits in Gothenburg in 2000 and Gleneagles in 2005 are exclusively mentioned by anti-capitalist activists, and other counter-summits are much more prominent in their narratives, especially the counter-summit in Prague in 2000 (see Figure 2.4). As in Italy, German anti-capitalist activists consider the counter-summit in Prague to be an additional peak GJM event – next to the counter-summits in Seattle, Genoa and Heiligendamm – that brought together groups from various backgrounds and created a new concept of protest (with different marches – see also Juris, 2008; Chesters & Welsh, 2004). Also the counter-summit in Heiligendamm in 2007 is more prominent among anti-capitalist activists (see Figure 2.4), who in particular stress the event's role in building and reinforcing new radical left networks in Germany. Similar to Italian anti-capitalist activists, German activists also stress the role of growing autonomist networks in the late 1990s in preparing the GJM's peak in terms of horizontal organisation and transnational cooperation. Activists in this context refer in particular to the European Zapatista network starting with a first international meeting in Chiapas (Mexico) in 1996 and the anti-racist no-border camps in the late 1990s (see Figure 2.4).

Also in Poland, counter-summits overall play a more central role in the narratives from anti-capitalist activists. Especially the counter-summits in Prague, Genoa and Heiligendamm are more prominent (see Figure 2.6). Anti-capitalist activists highlight in particular the role of the counter-summit in Prague in the build-up towards the GJM's peak more than other activists. The events in Prague are described as a central impulse for later mobilisations especially since they strengthened transnational ties and had an important influence on Polish activists, in particular on anarchists' move from sub-cultural activities to more social issues (see chapter 3). Furthermore, anti-capitalist activists tend to consider the counter-summit in Heiligendamm in 2007 more central to the GJM than activists from the anti-neoliberal sector. In addition, Polish anti-capitalist activists also hold the counter-summits in Seattle in 1999 and in Warsaw in 2004 – while more frequently mentioned by anti-neoliberal activists (see Figure 2.6) – to have had more incisive effects: the counter-summit in Seattle is described as a first glimpse of the larger, global movement, the counter-summit in Warsaw with respect to its capacity to mobilise a broad range of activists. And similar to anti-capitalist activists in

Italy and Germany, anti-capitalist activists in Poland stress the role of no-border camps (but not Zapatista networks) in building transnational activist ties in Europe in the late 1990s and early 2000s, in particular anarchist activists.

Linked to the centrality of counter-summits in anti-capitalist activists' narratives, counter-summits also play a more prominent role in these activists' perception of the movements' decline than in other sectors. As mentioned above in the Italian case, anti-capitalist activists tend to stress the detrimental effect of repression during the counter-summit in Genoa and the divisions it created within the movement more so than anti-neoliberal and eco-pacifist activists. The events in Genoa are in particular described to have rendered the movement too defensive. The GJM's decline, hence, is understood to have already started after Genoa (see also Zamponi & Daphi, 2014).

Similarly, German anti-capitalist activists attribute the decline of the movement more to the role of repression than do anti-neoliberal and eco-pacifist activists, especially in the context of the counter-summit in Genoa, but also following the counter-summit, for example in Gleneagles in 2005. Anti-capitalist activists in both Italy and Germany put this development in the context of an overall increase in repression from the early 2000s onwards, which is also linked to the aftermath of the 9/11 attacks, with the increased police violence creating an atmosphere of fear that inhibited political mobilisation. Also, summits are reported to be increasingly difficult to reach because they are held in more remote places. With respect to the protests in Genoa, German activists additionally stress that radical perspectives on global justice afterwards lost weight due to the dominance of *Attac* in Germany. German anti-capitalist activists, similar to anti-capitalist activists in Italy, see the GJM declining after Genoa; however, in contrast to their Italian counterparts, German anti-capitalist activists identify a new peak after low levels of mobilisation, namely the counter-summit in Heiligendamm.

Also for anti-capitalist activists in Poland, counter-summits – or rather their aftermath – play a more crucial role in the decline of the GJM than for other activists. Anti-capitalist activists in Poland, contrary to anti-neoliberal activists, stress how divisions re-emerging after the counter-summit in Warsaw between different radical left and within anarchist groups contributed to the decline of the movement.

Central Events within the Anti-neoliberal and Eco-pacifist Sector

In narratives by activists from the *anti-neoliberal and eco-pacifist sectors*, other events play a more prominent role. In particular the ESFs and the WSFs as well as the anti-war demonstrations in 2003 are more central here than in the anti-capitalist sector. In Italy, anti-neoliberal and especially eco-pacifist activists more prominently refer to the WSF in Porto Alegre in 2001, the ESF in Florence in 2002 and the anti-war demonstrations in 2003 (see Figure 2.2). Anti-neoliberal and eco-pacifist activists emphasise all three events more as peak events of the GJM than anti-capitalist activists do. They emphasise positive experiences of feeling belongingness and empowerment and stress the event's success in building broad coalitions. On top of Seattle, the first WSF in Porto Alegre in this vein is perceived to have provided the 'spirit' to overcome divisions in the left (I9/IT/EP-4; see full quote on p. 1). In preparing for the peak event, eco-pacifist activists additionally stress the important role of the international and Italian debt-relief campaign in the late 1990s in strengthening transnational activist networks (see Figure 2.1).

In Germany, it is particularly activists from the anti-neoliberal sector who refer most frequently to the first WSF in Porto Alegre, the ESF in Florence and the anti-war demonstrations (see Figure 2.4). Both anti-neoliberal and eco-pacifist activists consider the ESF in Florence and especially the first WSF in Porto Alegre as crucial peak events of the GJM. Furthermore, German eco-pacifist activists in contrast to both anti-neoliberal and anti-capitalist activists regard the anti-war demonstrations in 2003 as central events of the GJM's climax. Anti-neoliberal activists instead stress the role of protests against cuts in social services in 2004 (see the Introduction chapter) as part of the GJM's main phase (see also Figure 2.4). With respect to events prior to the climax, eco-pacifists also stress the international debt-relief campaigns linked to ecumenist international networks in the late 1990s as important first events that brought groups together internationally.

Also in Poland, the first WSF and the ESF in Florence have a more central role in anti-neoliberal activists' narratives (see also Figure 2.6). Anti-neoliberal activists hold the first WSF and the ESF in Florence to be influential early events more so than activists from the anti-capitalist sector (while these events overall are not as central in Polish narratives as in Italy and Germany; see the section 'Remembering the GJM in Poland'). These events, in particular the ESF in Florence, are perceived to have intensified transnational activist exchanges and networks. With respect to the ESF in Florence, especially anti-neoliberal activists stress the large Polish delegations that went there, and some mention the impulses the event provided for the anti-war demonstrations a year later (also taking place in Poland). Among the peak events, the anti-war protests play a more central role in anti-neoliberal narratives, in contrast to their anti-capitalist counterparts, as anti-neoliberal activists stress these protests' ability to mobilise diverse groups. In this vein, a number of anti-neoliberal activists even describe a decline of mobilisations after the anti-war demonstrations (despite the larger counter-summit in Warsaw a year later; see the Introduction chapter).

In connection to the centrality of the WSFs and the ESFs in anti-neoliberal activists' narratives, these meetings also play a larger role in the activists' description of the movement's decline. In Italy, Germany and Poland, activists in particular stress the role of the weakening ESFs in the overall decline of the GJM. Over the years, the ESFs are considered to have weakened as they lost the capacity to bring different activist groups together, with disagreements growing, for example, between NGOs and radical left groups. Participation accordingly decreased, especially since the third ESF in London in 2004. In addition, I have shown above how in each country anti-neoliberal activists consider other events more central in the movement's decline than anti-capitalist activists because they affected their sector more directly. In Italy this concerns the role of the centre-left government in creating divisions within the movement, namely with the communist party PRC involved in that government. Polish anti-neoliberal activists in this context stress in particular the divisions within the Polish chapter of *Attac* as central to the GJM's downfall. And among German anti-neoliberal activists, the growing public awareness about global injustices linked to the success of *Attac* is seen to contribute to the GJM's end.

CONCLUSION

This first empirical chapter illuminated how diverse activists' narratives about the GJM can be with respect to the actors and events they consider central. I identified both country- and sector-specific patterns in this regard. Activists most prominently refer to events and actors closest to them both geographically and ideologically. This includes not only events and actors that actually took place in activists' respective regions and sectors but also those *perceived* as closer, highlighting how national and sectorial differences are not random, but correspond with group-specific meaning making. This chapter accordingly showed the different ways in which events can be interpreted – as beginnings or ends, as successes or failures, as significant or marginal. I first showed how activists' views of central events and actors of the GJM vary considerably between Italy, Germany and Poland. In doing so, this chapter underlined the significance of national and local contexts in transnational social movements (see the Introduction chapter). In addition to national differences, I also identified transnational patterns in activists' narratives as activists shared perspectives on central events and actors within each sectors across the three countries. Such transnational narrative patterns will be further explored in the following chapter by examining such transnational commonalities beyond the individual sectors.

National Differences

As I have shown, there are considerable national differences in activists' narratives. Activists' narratives focus on national GJM developments; hence, the actors and events regarded as relevant are largely based within their respective country or region, most prominently in Poland. The counter-summit in Genoa in 2001, for example, is central only to Italian and German activists. Despite these differences, certain events are central to activists in all three countries, especially the counter-summit in Seattle in 1999. I also identified differences between the three countries with respect to the degree of congruence: activists agree on primary actors and events more in some cases (especially in Italy) and less in others (especially in Poland). This means that agreement diverges about the boundaries of the movement with respect to the spectrum of groups involved and the time span of activities. Such differences in narrative congruence largely correspond with the intensity of sectorial links within each country (these links being highest in Italy and lowest in Poland; see the Introduction chapter).

Along with the overall larger congruence of narratives, Italian activists focus on a smaller selection of events, most prominently the counter-summit in Genoa (2001), and a shorter time span of the GJM between 1999 and 2004. Despite its significantly lower numbers of participants, the counter-summit in Genoa stands out in Italian narratives and is understood as a watershed in terms of revealing both the strengths and the weaknesses of the GJM. Furthermore, Italian activists, in contrast to their German and Polish counterparts, clearly identify the causes and timing of the GJM's decline after 2004. In addition to the strong repression during the Genoan counter-summit, activists particularly consider that the incapacity of the anti-war demonstrations in 2003 to stop the war in Iraq and the plans to form a centre-left government in Italy from 2004 onwards have contributed to the GJM's decline. With respect to the central GJM actors, Italian activists include a broad spectrum of groups in their narratives. In particular, activists connected to the *Centri Sociali*, the Catholic and secular peace and solidarity groups as well as grassroots unions are regarded as central. Compared to Germany, especially the role of trade unions stands out in Italian narratives; and compared to Poland, the contribution of Catholic peace and solidarity groups is very prominent.

In Germany, activists include a broader range of relevant GJM events in their narratives than in Italy. They also identify a longer duration of the GJM – from the protests against the MAI agreement in 1998 to the G8 summit in Heiligendamm in 2007. In addition to the counter-summit in Heiligendamm, all activists consider in particular the counter-summits in Seattle in 1999 and in Genoa in 2001 to be main GJM events. In contrast to the Italian case, the causes of the decline of the GJM are less clearly and coherently identified in German narratives. Activists in Germany attribute the GJM's end after 2007 either to a general fatigue or the need for new alliances and forms of mobilisation in the context of the financial crisis. More moderate activists additionally attribute the GJM's decline to the overall success of its claims in terms of entering mainstream politics. With respect to actors, German activists focus on a few groups, particularly *Attac Germany*. Beyond *Attac* and the IL as well as some environmental groups, activists tend to disagree on how central other groups were to the GJM in Germany. In contrast to Italy and Poland, in particular environmental groups stand out in German narratives; in contrast to Poland in addition NGOs are very prominent.

In Poland, activists focus on a few events within a relatively long GJM time frame between 1999 and 2008. Activists regard as particularly central the labour struggles in 2001 and 2002, the anti-war protests in 2003 and the demonstrations against the Economic Forum in Warsaw in 2004. With the exception of the counter-summit in Prague in 2001, transnational GJM events play a noticeably more minor role in Polish narratives than in Italian and especially German accounts. Furthermore, Polish activists disagree on the causes and timing of the decline of the GJM more than activists in Italy as well as in Germany. Aside from the new conditions for mobilisation with the financial crisis from 2007 onwards, activists in Poland largely disagree on the reasons for the GJM's decline. With respect to actors, Polish activists mention a broad range of groups, but only very few of them are considered to be principle across sectors. Across sectors, activists hold in particular anarchist and anarcho-syndicalist groups as well as small feminist and environmental groups to be important. In contrast to Italy and Germany, the prominence of anarchist activists and the absence of faith-based and secular solidarity groups are especially striking in Polish narratives.

Sectorial Differences

Furthermore, I have demonstrated that views on central events and actors also differ between sectors. These sectorial patterns are similar across all three countries: activists refer most prominently and most explicitly to events and groups closest to them in terms of organisation, ideas and tactics. My analysis revealed in particular differences between the more radical activists from the anti-capitalist sector and the more moderate activists from the anti-neoliberal and eco-pacifist sectors.

With respect to groups, I showed how anti-capitalist activists refer more prominently to radical left groups and include a broader variety of them. Likewise, anti-capitalist activists are the only ones to mention certain radical left groups, for example, the *Giovani Comunisti* in Italy and the PGA network in both Italy and Germany. Anti-neoliberal activists in turn consider moderate left groups to be more central, and these activists in all three countries stress the role of *Attac* and established unions more than activists from other sectors do. In Germany and Poland, anti-neoliberal activists also highlight the role of left parties as well as organisations linked to them more than other activists. Eco-pacifist activists in Italy and Germany in contrast tend to regard environmental NGOs and faith-based groups as more central than activists from other sectors. Political parties and especially trade unions in contrast are considered much less significant by eco-pacifist activists.

I have, moreover, shown that events identified as prominent differ between more radical activists of the anti-capitalist sector, on the one hand, and more moderate activists of the anti-neoliberal and eco-pacifist sectors, on the other. Within narratives by anti-capitalist activists, counter-summits are credited with a much more major role in the GJM's growth as well as decline. In addition to putting more emphasis on counter-summits that other activists also consider central (especially those in Seattle in 1999, in Genoa in 2001, in Warsaw in 2004 and in Heiligendamm in 2007), anti-capitalist activists across countries refer to a broader range of counter-summits. In this vein, anti-capitalist activists in Italy almost exclusively mention the counter-summits in Prague in 2000 and in Naples in 2001; in Germany the same holds for the counter-summits in Gothenburg in 2000 and in Gleneagles in 2005, and in Poland it is likewise with respect to the counter-summit in Heiligendamm in 2007. Furthermore, anti-capitalist activists in all three countries stress the role of new networks of autonomist and anarchist activists developing in the 1990s in preparing the GJM's growth, especially with respect to European Zapatista networks and no-border camps. More moderate activists from the anti-neoliberal and eco-pacifist activists in contrast consider the ESFs and WSFs as well as the anti-war demonstrations more central events in both the GJM's growth and decline than anti-capitalist activists. With respect to the GJM's growth and success, especially the first WSF in Porto Alegre in 2001, the first ESF in Florence in 2002 and the anti-war demonstrations are highlighted across the three countries by moderate activists. And with respect to the GJM's decline, activists from the anti-neoliberal and eco-pacifist sectors especially stress the role of the deteriorating later ESFs.

Malleability of Narratives

To some extent the revealed differences in events and actors activists consider central across countries and sectors correspond to the different national and sectorial constellations of GJM mobilisations. Country- and sector-specific narratives, hence, partly depend on the country- and sector-specific experiences in which activists were involved. For example, *Attac* is a more central actor in German narratives since *Attac* indeed played a much more central role in the German GJM activities than in other countries. And trade unions are more central in Italian narratives because grassroots unions in particular were much more involved in the Italian GJM than in the other two countries. Also the different degrees of narrative congruence between Italy, Germany and Poland can be connected to the particular GJM constellation in each country, namely to the different degrees of intensity and longevity of cross-sectorial ties in the three countries – with the highest in Italy and the lowest in Poland (see the Introduction chapter).

On the other hand, the differences in activists' narratives are not only due to a different 'objective' exposure to a certain environment, but also depend on group-specific meaning making, highlighting the malleability of activists' narratives. Narratives are not simply a matter of adding up past events in the respective country or sector; they are rather actively constructed through a selection that excludes certain events and highlights others. In this vein, this chapter's analysis has shown that activists also neglect certain events and actors even though they were geographically or ideologically close and highlight others despite being more remote. This became evident, on the one hand, with respect to the sectorial patterns in activists' narratives identified in this chapter revealing how certain events are given importance beyond the immediate national or regional relevance. For example, Italian anti-capitalist activists consider the largest mobilisations in Italy – the anti-war demonstrations and the first ESF in Florence – to be less significant than the counter-summit in Genoa. Similarly, Polish and German anti-capitalist activists tend to de-emphasise the importance of the anti-war protests in 2003 in their respective countries. Anti-neoliberal activists in turn tend to neglect various large counter-summits despite their occurrence within – or close to – their respective countries, for example, in Italy regarding the counter-summit in Naples in 2001, in Germany with respect to the counter-summit in Prague in 2000 and in Poland regarding the counter-summit in Heiligendamm in 2007.

On the other hand, the malleability of narratives became evident with respect to the changes in the centrality of groups and events over time. In this vein, some events and groups that were in fact marginal at the time were rather prominent in activists' retrospective narratives in 2011/2012. This concerns, for example, the protests in Seattle in narratives by German activists: Originally the counter-summit in Seattle was little noticed in Germany (see Introduction chapter), but in retrospective narratives it is defined as a central first event. Similarly, Polish activists stress the role of the counter-summit in Seattle more than the one in Genoa in 2001, despite the fact that Seattle attracted little attention at the time and that notably more Polish activists participated in the protests in Genoa. Furthermore, some events and groups that used to be relatively prominent at the time tend to be neglected in the retrospective narratives. For example, the strong focus in Italian narratives on the events in Genoa tends to neglect other developments and events, both prior and later ones, for instance, the counter-summit in Nice in 2000 and the ESF in Florence in 2002. Likewise, Polish activists' retrospective emphasis on national mobilisations against neoliberal policies de-emphasises the role of international GJM events, despite Polish activists' considerable participation in them. Furthermore, also certain groups lose visibility in retrospect. The German narratives' focus on the group *Attac* in particular tends to overlook the role that other groups played, in particular grassroots groups linked to PGA and BUKO. Italian and Polish narratives comparably focus on certain actors at the expense of others; in Italy this particularly concerns the *Centri Sociali* and grassroots unions, and in Poland it especially refers to the anarchist groups.

NOTES

1. The quantitative analysis draws on a selection of five interviews per national sector (with the exception of the Polish eco-pacifist sector due to its minor role; see details in appendix A). The selection was based on the criterion of (a) variety of different groups within each sector and (b) activists' feeling of belongingness to the GJM at large (for details on interviewee selection, see chapter 1).

2. Overall, the continuities identified with respect to anti-austerity mobilisations are less prominent in Italy than in Germany and Poland, which most probably is connected to the earlier timing of interviews in Italy: When interviews were conducted with Italian activists in the first half of 2011, these mobilisations had recently started.

3. These disputes mainly concerned attacks on the police during the kick-off demonstration (for more details about this dispute, see Teune, 2012).

Chapter 3

The Shared GJM Narrative

It was as if from different observation points everyone started walking on their own, without knowing that the others were walking as well, and once arrived started discovering that it was possible to arrive at the same place but walking through different paths. (I5/IT/AN-14)

Do activists tell similar stories about the GJM beyond country- and sector-specific differences? This is the question this chapter addresses. Hence, in contrast to the previous chapter, this second empirical chapter explores the commonalities rather than differences in activists' GJM narratives across countries and sectors. Examining such shared narrative patterns provides crucial insights into the formation of movement identity, as I elaborated in chapter 1, since collective narratives about a shared past can create a notion of shared experience that is central to defining commonalities and attributing agency to the movement.

I will show below that while activists in Italy, Germany and Poland emphasise different events and actors, they nonetheless share a transnational 'GJM narrative'. As I will elaborate, activists across countries and sectors order the various GJM experiences into a shared plot. This plot comprises a sequence of four episodes, and while events within each episode are not necessarily the same, the characteristics attributed to each are strikingly similar across countries and sectors (see Table 3.1). Activists in this vein identify (1) a situation prior to the GJM's beginning, which is characterised by a weak and divided left and the hegemony of neoliberalism; (2) a build-up episode in which the GJM starts to grow in terms of transnational cooperation, but is limited in its success to overcome divisions in the left and to challenge neoliberal hegemony; (3) a peak episode in which the GJM reaches its full potential and succeeds in overcoming neoliberal hegemony and divisions among the left;

Table 3.1   The GJM Narrative's Four Episodes

Episodes	Main characteristics	Main GJM events		
		Italy	Germany	Poland
A 'desert' before our time	• Divisions in the left • Neoliberal hegemony	–	–	–
The build-up: Lessons in joint mobilisation	• Continuing divisions • Limited public response • Growing transnational ties • Lessons in horizontal organisation	Anti-war 1999 Seattle 1999	MAI campaign 1998 Cologne 1999	(Seattle 1999) Prague 2000 Work struggles 2001–2003
The GJM's peak: Succeeding in joint mobilisation	• Overcoming divisions in the left • Challenging neoliberal hegemony	Genoa 2001 ESF 2002 Anti-war 2003	Seattle 1999 Genoa 2001 Heiligendamm 2007	Anti-war 2003 Warsaw 2004
The end: Declining mobilisation	• Return to sectors • Back to the local	After 2004	After 2007	After 2007/2008

and (4) the GJM's decline and end as marked by its decreasing capacity for cross-sectorial and transnational mobilisation.

I will reveal how this shared plot integrates the different country- and sector-specific experiences and perspectives. Crucially, it creates a sense of shared experience, of collective hardship and triumph that outlines central commonalities within the GJM with respect to cognitions, boundaries and emotional proximity. In particular the shared experiences of successfully challenging neoliberal hegemony and overcoming divisions within the left underline the GJM's master frame of anti-neoliberalism, its difference to previous and later movements and the shared feelings of disappointment and joy.

This chapter combines a structural with a content analysis of activists' narratives (see details in chapter 1). In this vein, the composite analysis focuses on recurrent combinations of events and evaluations, that is, patterns in how major GJM events (see chapter 2) are *evaluated* both in the sense of direct interpretations and with respect to their position within the overall sequence of events. Among the sixty-seven activist interviews in total, this chapter draws on a selection of forty-seven interviews along with the focus groups in each country. The interview selection concentrates on those activists who count themselves as part of the GJM at large (in contrast to the interviews analysed in chapter 4).

A 'DESERT' BEFORE OUR TIME

Activists' narratives across all sectors and countries clearly contrast the GJM with the situation prior to its beginning. This situation is characterised in particular by a weak left and the hegemony of neoliberal thought and policies (see Table 3.1). Activists consider both aspects to be related since neoliberal hegemony draws on as well as fosters a weak left. In this vein, activists describe the 1980s and 1990s as a 'desert' (I15/IT/AC-8), a 'valley of tears' (I24/DE/AC-14) and 'a vacuum' (I2/PL/AN-47). This contrast clearly delineates the GJM's characteristics and its boundaries as the stress on previous divisions highlights the GJM's ability to build broad coalitions and the emphasis on neoliberal hegemony underlines the GJM's successful challenge of this paradigm. The differentiation exaggerates the weakness of the left prior to the GJM and neglects some prominent left mobilisations in the previous decades, including earlier protests against trade agreements as well as pro-democratic movements around the world. Also, prominent movements in Italy, Germany and Poland tend to be overlooked in this context: Polish activists are remarkably silent about the famous *Solidarność* movement in the 1970s and 1980s, as are German activists with respect to protests against Soviet rule in East Germany. Furthermore, Italian as well as German activists mention the '68 movements in their respective countries only in the context of highlighting differences to the GJM.

Divisions in the Left

Activists clearly differentiate the GJM from the internal divisions that characterised the left in prior decades and contrast these divisions with the GJM's broad coalition work. Italian activists accordingly describe the 1980s and 1990s as 'years of defeat' (I16/IT/AC-23) with 'very heavy' divisions (I5/IT/AN-14) and 'violent relations between sectors' (I15/IT/AC-48) in which different left groups were not able to cooperate and achieve a unified 'fighting front' (I4/IT/AN-4). Conflicts ensuing from the '68 movement in Italy are seen to play a notable role in such divides. More moderate activists in this respect especially stress the role of the 1970s' 'counter-productive' violence (I9/IT/EP-88) in creating divides, while more radical activists highlight the role of repression and the 'criminalisation of direct action' (I18/IT/AC-24) in those years. Across sectors, activists consider left divisions to have continued well into the late 1990s until the take off of the GJM, as the following quote illustrates: '[The counter-summit in Genoa] goes beyond a whole series of dichotomies in which Italy was trapped during the 1980s, like between violence and non-violence which would then become real ideologies, self-constructed ghettos' (FG/IT/ACb-15).

Similarly, activists in Germany contrast the GJM most prominently with conflicts between moderate and radical left groups in the 1968 German movement. The 1960s and 1970s in this way are considered a period of constant 'turf battles' (I2/DE/AN-45) and 'dreadful clashes' (I20/DE/AC-43) between different left groups such as social democrats, Trotskyists, Maoists, anarchists and autonomist groups. Such divisions are described to have continued into the 1980s and were reinforced in the 1990s in the context of the end of state socialism making coalitions between these 'unthinkable' (I23/DE/AC-6), as also noted by an *Attac* activist:

> The painful history of the Western left is strongly characterised by battles against each other. ... In the 60s and 70s this was the dominant way to communicate between left groups, that you would ruin each other's events and break each other's heads. (FG/DE/AN-47)

Polish activists, in contrast to their German and Italian counterparts, focus on divisions emerging from political transformation from 1989 onwards in Poland. While Soviet rule is also described to have considerably weakened civil society, after transformation the left is particularly seen to have 'collapsed due to its bad connotations with the past' (I7/PL/AN-4). Activists elaborate how 'anti-communist propaganda' (I3/PL/AN-84) and sentiment was very prominent in those years and how it made left criticism of neoliberal capitalism very difficult as it 'smells like communism' (I15/PL/AC-11) and is accused of 'end[ing] in Gulags' (I6/PL/AN-48). Activists highlight strong divisions between left groups prior to the GJM, especially between anarchist, communist, socialist and Trotskyist groups as well as with more reformist left groups. These divisions are regarded to have continued well into the late 1990s, leaving the left 'completely atomised' (I2/PL/AN-35) and 'really very weak' (I16/PL/AC-6). An anarchist activist in this vein describes how divisions continued till 2000: 'I think only around 2000 this border which was quite clear started to blur, so it was like 10 years where [you] would either be a socialist or communist ... or anarchist'. (I18/PL/AC-6)

Neoliberal Hegemony

In addition to divisions within the left, GJM activists also stress the predominance of neoliberal thought prior to the GJM. Accordingly, activists connect the weakness of the left not only to internal conflicts, but also to the generally unconducive environment of 'neoliberal hegemony'. Activists describe how after the end of Cold War a process of ideological homogenisation took place in which the 'virus' (FG/PL/AN-102) of neoliberalism diffused rapidly and became the only legitimate way of thinking with 'unsurpassable ... arrogance' (I9/DE/EP-55) and with seriously detrimental effects on people's lives. If mentioned at all, mobilisations against neoliberal institutions and policies prior to the GJM, for example, the protests against the IMF and World Bank meeting in Berlin in 1988 (see chapter 2), are perceived to have been limited in their ability to fundamentally question the legitimacy of neoliberalism owing to their focus on specific topics, sectors and regions.

Activists in Italy and Germany in this way describe how the predominance of the 'neoliberal system' (I11/IT/EP-15) had a notably detrimental effect on the left. It was a 'shot in the neck for the left' (I22/DE/AC-8) as it left no room for alternatives to neoliberal capitalism. Activists across sectors in particular talk about the paradigm of the supposed lack of alternatives in that period linked to Francis Fukuyama's theory (1992) of the 'end of history' and the 'TINA principle' (There Is No Alternative) coined by the former prime minister of the United Kingdom Margaret Thatcher and picked up by later politicians. Accounts from both Italy and Germany highlight this notion:

Some aspects ... were previously considered as something definitive, [in particular] 'the history is over, the end of history' of the first 1990s and the neoliberal capitalistic order .... And in that moment [questioning] this was something which was not at all obvious because that neoliberal order looked like a paradisiacal condition. Everybody would tell us that the world was just, happy and serene. (I19/IT/AC-46)

So, the experience ... in the 90s of the complete collapse of all larger left [groups], this experience of [the German chancellor] Schröder's dictum 'there is no alternative', this in fact was the spirit of the left in the 90s. (I12/DE/EP-23)

In Poland, activists link neoliberal hegemony more specifically to the consequences of Polish transformation after 1989 (see also chapter 2). The introduction of neoliberal policies 'from above' (I1/PL/AN-4) in the 1990s is described as a 'shock-therapy' (I2/PL/AN-9), considerably deteriorating the Poles' previous levels of social security. The elite of the *Solidarność* movement is largely made responsible for this deterioration, having 'sold out' (I15/PL/AC-8) to the free-market economy in a 'complete betrayal' (I6/PL/AN-28). Activists elaborate on how the majority of Poles was 'seduced by the ideology of neoliberalism' (I3/PL/AN-37), believing that 'this legend of free market' (FG/PL/AN-28) was 'the best option for them' (I18/PL/AC-25). This mindset is considered to have made it very difficult to criticise neoliberal capitalism as it meant that the 'old left language described ... nothing any-more' (I2/PL/AN-47). An activist from an anarcho-syndicalist group concurs:

After '89 it sort of became almost unthinkable to criticize capitalism. ... The illusions at the beginning were really strong and even the people who were the most excluded from the system still believed ... in this myth of the trickle-down economy .... It was unheard of to say [that you did not believe in] this. (I15/PL/AC-8)

THE BUILD-UP: LESSONS IN JOINT MOBILISATION

As the book's previous chapter has shown, activists identify different starting points of the GJM. While the specific starting events differ, activists characterise these events in very similar ways. Events of the GJM's build-up are described as crucial lessons in joint mobilisation (see Table 3.1). Activists consider them as important first attempts towards empowerment and as partial successes in building a broad movement while challenging neoliberal hegemony. In particular, successes in building transnational ties and in discovering and developing horizontal forms of organisation are highlighted (see also Daphi, 2014b). At the same time, these events are associated, in contrast to the GJM's peak events, with failures and disappointments. Activists especially emphasise how cross-sectorial cooperation did not yet fully work out and how low and negative public attention to the movement's claims was due to the prevalence of neoliberal thought. Left divisions and neoliberal hegemony hence are not thought to be overcome in this episode. However, activists consider these initial setbacks to be valuable lessons in the lead-up to the GJM's peak. In underlining the initial failures, in fact, activists stress the GJM's later success and evoke a sense of shared past experiences of failure and frustration.

Next to sector-specific events (see chapter 2), activists across sectors also characterise other early events in the way described above: in Italy primarily the demonstrations against the war in Kosovo in 1999 and the counter-summit in Seattle in 1999; in Germany the counter-summit in Cologne in 1999 and the campaign against the Multilateral Agreement on Investment (MAI) in 1998; and in Poland the counter-summit in Prague in 2000 and the local work-related protests in the early 2000s (see chapter 2). While limited, these events are regarded as important first victories that kicked off the movement. German activists in this vein stress the 'victory' (I9/DE/EP-59) of 'successfully stopping' (I25/DE/AC-7) the MAI agreement, describing it as 'the first agreement that we brought down' (FG/DE/EP-51). Polish activists see the protests in Prague as a 'political rebirth' (I20/PL/AC-62) and the work struggles as 'an important moment' for GJM mobilisations in Poland (I3/PL/AN-16). And Italian activists consider the counter-summit in Seattle as the 'beginning of real contestation' (I5/IT/AN-2) and 'the straw that breaks the camel's back' (FG/IT/EP-10), as also noted by an activist from a *Centro Sociale* in southern Italy:

> We never felt the tide [of "new politics"] as we could feel [it] after Seattle when people were able to really stop [the summit]. And I think it was a sort of feeling that grew up starting from it. (I16/IT/AC-23)

Continuing Divisions

Across sectors and countries, activists reckon that the events of the build-up episode did not yet bridge divisions in the left. In this way, activists in Italy stress with respect to demonstrations against the Kosovo War in the late 1990s that while different groups did come together, central cleavages between different sectors were not yet overcome. Moderate activists in this context, for example, recall their indignation that activists from the *Centri Sociali* 'would absolutely shamelessly negotiate ... with the policemen to have a little kerfuffle for the press' (I7/IT/EP-53). And also more radical activists stress how internal conflicts continued in this campaign, as the following quote illustrates:

> [In the protests against the Kosovo War] large parts of different groups and experiences ... were together, ... of course it was not ... exactly the Genoa process ... it did not help Italian politics to really leave its internal fighting, its local fighting. (I16/IT/AC-8)

Similarly, German activists recall how the different activist milieus did not work well together during the counter-summit in Cologne in 1999.

Activists describe the mobilisation as 'not successful' (I2/DE/AN-10) since 'no dynamic evolved' (I12/DE/EP-12) between the different groups and 'coalition work went wrong' (I24/DE/AC-8). Next to existing divisions, the decision of the German government – led by a coalition of Social Democratic Party (SPD) and the green party *Bündnis 90/die Grünen* – to support the NATO's intervention in the Balkan wars is seen to have led to additional ruptures within the moderate left. The low numbers of participants due to these splits are considered a 'dreadful disappointment' (I23/DE/AC-10). An activist from an anti-fascist group summarises this view:

> The coalition back then [in Cologne] did not work out; it classically diverged then into a left-radical and autonomist milieu and into a, let's say, moderate left milieu centred around NGOs among others. And also this, back then, did not correspond with the … later GJM, where one did politics together across diverse ideological borders. And '99 was so to say a point in time, where all this did not work out yet. (I24/DE/AC-8)

Also activists in Poland highlight the continuing divisions during the counter-summit in Prague (while the event is seen to help overcome them later on; see chapter 2) and the limits of cooperation during the work struggles between 2001 and 2003. While considered important in connecting issues of global neoliberalism with local working conditions for the first time, the work struggles and in particular the prominent strike at the cable factory in Ożarów in 2002 are described as a 'focus for a moment' (I19/PL/AC-108) rather than a lasting event in terms of activist coalitions and political impact as well as limited to 'groups more into social economic issues' (I3/PL/AN-46). Activists likewise stress that during the counter-summit in Prague, anarchist and communist groups 'mobilised independently' (I19/PL/AC-146), and others underline that primarily anarchist groups were involved, as the following quote reveals:

> It was the Prague protests that brought some groups from Poland [together] and I think they were mainly anarchists, but this was almost a year after the Seattle events and as far as I remember, this was when this anti-globalism came close to us, yeah before it was far away. (I3/PL/AN-52)

Limited Public Response

Activists furthermore highlight how public attention to events of the build-up episode was low and largely negative because public opinion was shaped by the prevalence of neoliberal thinking. Italian activists in this way emphasise the overall ignorance of the issue of global economy in Italy prior to the counter-summit in Genoa, in particular in the context of the counter-summit in Seattle. In this vein, several activists stress how they discovered the significance of the events in Seattle and the issues raised by it before other actors did so. For example, an activist from a peace group recalls how 'the people in Lilliput were the first ones who understood the importance of Seattle' in challenging the world's 'dysfunctional economic order' (I7/IT/EP-20). Similarly, an activist from the communist party PRC recalls how he was the first within his party to realise the event's significance:

> I can remember, in Italy people were very surprised about the dimension and harshness of the fights and the strength of this contestation [in Seattle]. I remember that I personally sent a female comrade to follow what was going on in Seattle ... and I remember that the administration of the party came to me asking: 'Why do you want to send her over there? It is too expensive, we will read everything online'. ... I am saying this to show you that there was a widespread underestimation of the event. I remember I organised something [on international commerce] here, in central Rome, but just a few people came. (I4/IT/AN-4)

German activists similarly describe with respect to the counter-summit in Cologne in 1999 how media attention was low or largely negative. The fact that this event was 'difficult to communicate to the public' (I12/DE/EP-12) is considered a result of both the missing collaboration between left groups – with each doing different activities – and the omnipresence of neoliberal thinking. In his way, an autonomist activist highlights her disappointment about the lack in public interest in the Cologne protests:

> For me [the counter-summit in Cologne] was the worst, politically really the most dreadful for me. But it was also this time; it was during the Yugoslav Wars and everyone was attuned to the TINA principle. Well, we held a national press conference. One intern took part in this and cried afterwards; she found [the lack in public interest] so dreadful. ... And the critique of capitalism did not get through ... it did not work out making them [the protests] visible. (I20/DE/AC-33)

Also Polish activists stress the missing attention to early GJM events abroad in Polish media; they particularly report the misrepresentation of these events in the context of the counter-summits not only in Prague, but also in Seattle and Genoa. Activists highlight the very low public interest in anti-neoliberalism in Poland 'as the mainstream media would avoid ... the Seattle events' (I3/PL/AN-68). They also emphasise the strong misrepresentation of these events by Polish media, describing activists as 'terrorists' (FG/PL/AN-26) and 'beasts' (I17/PL/AC-22) and failing to report the protests' goals and ideas. The following quote outlines this view:

As the alterglobalist movements ... appeared in the world, Seattle, Genoa and things like that, it was treated very badly ... by the press [in Poland]. I mean they were perceived as kind of hooligans, who actually don't know what they want, ... are radical ... there were very different accusations against them. (I6/PL/AN-44)

Growing Transnational Ties

Activists identify build-up events as a sizable contribution to establishing and strengthening transnational ties – both in the sense of personal contacts with activists from abroad and with respect to a global analysis of problems. Activists describe the experience of people coming together from all over the world during protests as something new and inspiring. This exchange is considered to have strengthened a global approach, meaning the understanding that local problems form a part of global developments.

Activists associate several sector-specific build-up events with growing transnational ties, as chapter 2 showed, for example, anti-capitalist activists refer to the meetings of the European Zapatista networks in this context and eco-pacifist activists to the international debt-relief campaign. In addition, Italian activists across sectors consider the counter-summit in Seattle as well as the protests against the war in Kosovo to have notably strengthened transnational ties. The protests against the Kosovo War accordingly are described as a 'starting point [for] a global approach to Italian politics' (I16/IT/AC-6). The protests in Seattle are similarly associated with the 'birth of a new language to portray conflicts' (I18/IT/AC-8) and the discovery of an 'international movement' (I1/IT/AN-1) more generally. In addition to a global approach, activists highlight the increasing interaction with activists from other countries and the new insights and activities such exchange triggered. Following this, an activist from a *Centro Sociale* in Rome stresses how the concept of a global day of action in Seattle was new to her group and how Indian peasant movements inspired them to participate in the context of protests against the *Food and Agriculture Organization* (FAO) in 1999 in Rome:

[Indian peasant movements] were going to Seattle in November, and ... they were inviting us to either go or organise something on that day because there was a global day of action. And ... that was completely new and I remember during that meeting we looked around and said 'Seattle? November?' people going from all over the world, it was like weird. It wasn't standard. (I17/IT/AC-10)

Similarly, activists in Germany describe the counter-summit in Cologne as well as the protests against the MAI agreement as crucial in increasing transnational ties and 'opening up the horizon' (I13/DE/EP-33). With respect to Cologne, activists for example stress the motivation to 'get to know each other internationally' (I24/DE/AC-66). The intensifying exchange between activists in different countries and continents during these events is considered to have helped in defining a 'global frame' (I5/DE/AN-10) to address problems of neoliberalism. This way, activists emphasise how the protests against the MAI agreement brought together activists from different countries, including movements from the 'Global South, be it south-Korean unionists or … peasant organisations from Latin America' (I25/DE/AC-11), and how it facilitated a global approach, as also the following quote underlines, (while focusing on partners in the Global North): 'The first … manifest way in which a central point was globally addressed was this MAI campaign, in which we participated together with other NGOs from Canada to the U.S., and France' (I2/DE/AN-8).

Polish activists stress the growing transnational cooperation particularly in the context of the counter-summit in Prague in 2000. The events in Prague are described to have helped recognise the global context as activists started to feel 'part of a broader movement' (I20/PL/AC-8) and enjoyed 'a culture of demonstration' from 'all over the world' (I2/PL/AN-21). The experience of 'mobilising internationally' (I19/PL/AC-6) in Prague is considered to be something new and to have confirmed the legitimacy of 'questioning the order' of neoliberalism in Poland (I1/PL/AN-5), as also noted by an anarchist activist: '[With] Prague, a kind of internationalisation of some Polish activists [took place] that had not been abroad beforehand' (I18/PL/AC-26).

Lessons in Horizontal Organisation

While divisions in the left are not considered overcome in build-up events, activists do stress the important lessons learned in horizontal organisation in these events linked to the transnational exchange. Activists underline the role of build-up events in reinventing the organisation and communication between political groups, going beyond 'traditional left discourse' (FG/IT/ACb-15). Activists underline the novelty of communicating 'equal to equal' (I12/PL/AN-52) and forming a network in which 'you don't lose yourselves in the link with others' (I16/IT/AC-52). This 'non-hierarchical organizing' (I20/DE/AC-49) is described as a new discovery and contrasted with the 'hierarchic' (I4/PL/AN-45) organisation in previous movements. In addition to sector-specific events characterised in this way (see chapter 2), also across sectors activists consider early events in this way, particularly in Italy and Poland.

Italian activists, in this vein, highlight how the counter-summit in Seattle introduced the GJM as 'the first movement without a centre' (FG/IT/ACb-15) and how this 'horizontalisation of political decisions' 'provided the Italian movements with ... elements of innovation' (I15/IT/AC-14). This form of organisation formed the 'central nucleus' that 'held things together' (I5/IT/AN-12). An activist from the grassroots union COBAS summarises accordingly:

> We discovered it [the GJM] first in Seattle .... And for the first time we discovered that it was possible to work together without one precise axis of strategy ... a lot of subjects could stay together and could work together without any hierarchy. And also that it was possible to decide without voting. I mean, who is the majority? ... For Italian people it was really strange. (I1/IT/AN-1)

German activists refer to lessons in horizontal organisation mainly in the context of sector-specific build-up events owing to the disappointment about the coalition work during the counter-summit in Cologne in 1999 (see above). Eco-pacifist activists in this context stress in particular the role of the international debt-relief campaigns in the late 1990s (see also chapter 2) in building 'open and plural platforms of mutual learning', which are considered to have manifested themselves later in the World and European Social Forums (I13/DE/EP-7) and their 'structureless and horizontal' organisation (I1/DE/AN-19). Anti-capitalist activists instead emphasise advances in horizontal organising in the context of Zapatista networks in Europe in the late 1990s as well as no-border camps (see chapter 2). An autonomist activist in this vein stresses how the Zapatistas furthered a new way of thinking about political mobilisation:

> If you consider it globally, then from the mid-90s onwards the Zapatistas arrived on the scene, who spelled out much more credibly and ... in depth [than the German squatters' movement in the 80s and early 90s] what a horizontal in contrast to a vertical ... form of organisation and intervention mean. (I25/DE/AC-10)

Similarly, Polish activists describe how in particular the counter-summit in Prague was a crucial inspiration for horizontal organisation in the Polish left contributing to 'a movement without hierarchical structures' (I16/PL/AC-23). In this vein, an activist from the Polish branch of *Attac* highlights: 'The Prague events left the very big imprint ... because that was the first time I realised yes, it is possible to work horizontally and work effectively, that never happened before' (I12/PL/AN-52).

THE GJM'S PEAK: SUCCEEDING IN JOINT MOBILISATION

Activists in all three countries identify peak events. Next to their size, activists characterise these events in a certain way; particularly, their ability to overcome left divides and successes in challenging neoliberal hegemony are stressed in contrast to build-up events (see also Daphi, 2014b). Peak events overall are evaluated very positively as they are primarily associated with the joys and successes of joint action, of feeling empowered and of being heard. In Italy such characterisation centrally concerns the counter-summit in Genoa in 2001, the European Social Forum (ESF) in Florence in 2002 and the anti-war demonstrations in 2003; in Germany it primarily concerns the counter-summits in Seattle in 1999 in Genoa and in Heiligendamm in 2007; and in Poland it concerns the anti-war demonstrations in 2003 and the counter-summit in Warsaw in 2004 (see Table 3.1 and chapter 2).

Activists contrast these peak events' successes both with the setbacks experienced in the build-up events (see the previous part) and with the situation previous to the GJM (see the section 'A "Desert" Before Our Time'). In this way, activists present events prior to the peak as lead-ups, as phrases such as 'it all confluxes in Genoa' (I18/IT/AC-14), 'on the path to Seattle' (I2/DE/AN-8) or 'the move to Warsaw' (I18/PL/AC-5) illustrate. Crucially, peak events are understood as turning points reversing the status quo with respect to neoliberal hegemony and left divisions, which stresses the GJM's agency.

Overcoming Divisions in the Left

Activists centrally link the size and success of the peak events to the movement's ability to bring together activist groups from different sectors around the joint frame of anti-neoliberalism. The defining characteristic of this episode is hence cross-sectorial cooperation instead of transnational cooperation as in the build-up events (see the previous part). Radical and moderate groups are described to have learned to cooperate in this context – with anti-capitalist activists stressing the necessity to get out of 'the ghetto' (I15/IT/AC-28, FG/DE/AC-23) and moderate activists highlighting the insight that a more fundamental critique of the 'whole construction of the global economic system' (I13/DE/EP-5) was necessary and that 'it's time to be against' the neoliberal system (I9/IT/EP-41).

Events in this episode are described as rich and inspiring experiences since building and being part of a broad movement are connected to feelings of joy, pride and triumph. Activists in particular emphasise the 'joyful' discovery (e.g., I2/PL/AN-21) and the 'great enthusiasm' (I25/DE/AC-48) of being among many and 'not alone' (e.g., I8/IT/EP-67) and how 'proud' (e.g., I18/IT/AC-18) everyone was of being able to coordinate the various groups in peak events regardless of differences. Activists also recall a notion of triumph about working together across differences *despite* the obstacles media and police created.

Italian activists consider especially the counter-summit in Genoa as a turning point in cross-sectorial cooperation.[1] Activists stress with respect to Genoa how different left groups joined forces that were unconnected or even in conflict before. Activists in this context describe how they realised that the 'reunification of a fighting front against one big enemy, the globalised capital' (I4/IT/AN-4) was necessary and possible. The events in Genoa are accordingly identified as the moment where 'you had stopped battling' (I8/IT/EP-32) and where activists came together in a 'sort of ecumenism … in which all of us, in some way were able to tolerate … the others' (I16/IT/AC-37). An activist from a Catholic organisation in this vein recalls:

> [In Genoa] there is a huge dialogue process among these realities that did not know each other beforehand. … Before I would not go to a social centre and the people of the social centre would not come to see me, a priest. … And now things change: we happened to be together … we were really understanding that the goal was uniting all of us. (I11/IT/EP-7)

German activists particularly stress the importance of the counter-summit in Seattle in increasing cross-sectorial cooperation. While only a handful of activists from Germany participated in the event (see the Introduction chapter), Seattle is seen as the beginning of a 'new kind of coalition between movements' (I5/DE/AN-10) in which 'different spectres worked hand-in-hand' (I20/DE/AC-36), representing 'the first broad resistance' (I13/DE/EP-13). Seattle in this way is contrasted with previous mobilisations, in particular with the counter-summit in Cologne, often with a note of triumph. The protests in Seattle are seen to have confirmed previous (largely failed) attempts to build a broad coalition and to have encouraged activists in Germany to continue mobilising. The counter-summit in Genoa in 2001 – in which several German activists participated – is considered a crucial additional impulse for such a broad coalition, especially for Europe and Germany. Activists accordingly describe how from Seattle onwards a broad coalition of left organisations emerged in Germany ranging 'from communist to Christian groups' (I1/DE/AN-29), 'characterised by the insight … that there isn't one truth, that there are different approaches to critique' (FG/DE/AN-47) This coalition is seen to have continued more or less until the counter-summit in Heiligendamm in 2007, where 'the different spectres got together again' (I20/DE/AC-43) and 'cooperated intensively' (I6/DE/AN-36). An activist from the post-autonomist network IL emphasises how the counter-summit in Seattle kicked off this broad coalition:

> And shortly after [the protests in Cologne] in fact came Seattle and we were laughing up our sleeves because we said 'this is exactly what we had in mind'. And we had bad luck with respect to Cologne … and we were right nonetheless and this is what Seattle made clear. … This circumstance … meant that we kept up the communication among a broad group ranging from church people, to

NGO people and to left radicals. This communication did not break down until Heiligendamm. (I23/DE/AC-11)

Polish activists connect the growth in cross-sectorial cooperation both to the anti-war protests in 2003 (primarily anti-neoliberal activists) and to the counter-summit in Warsaw in 2004 (primarily anti-capitalist activists) (see chapter 2). In this way, anti-neoliberal activists especially stress how during the 'high wave' (I7/PL/AN-6) of anti-war protests different groups cooperated, 'the communists with the hammer and a sickle on their banners, working together with anarchists, and more liberal human rights activists' (I3/PL/AN-70). And anti-capitalist activists particularly highlight how during the counter-summit in Warsaw 'different currents' worked together in a 'quite healthy coalition' (I19/PL/AC-25): anarchist with communist and Trotskyist groups as well as moderate unions and 'social democrats' (I6/PL/AN-8). NGOs are also described to have participated in this event, which before 'would [have been] simply frightened of joining this kind of crazy radicalism' (I18/PL/AC-51). An anarchist activist accordingly highlights the broad coalition during the Warsaw counter-summit:

> I would say that [the counter-summit in Warsaw] was the biggest moment for this movement in Poland. And that was the only moment when a lot of groups worked together ... I remember that a lot of groups, they went together to protests like anarchists together with some leftists and some communists and so on. (I17/PL/AC-9)

Challenging Neoliberal Hegemony

With respect to the peak events, activists describe at least a partial overcoming of the divisions within the left as well as the hegemonic neoliberal thinking prior to the GJM. Setting apart the era of unimpeded neoliberalism from the mobilisations of the GJM, activists define the GJM as a central actor in challenging neoliberal hegemony. Connected to this, the peak events are seen to have crucially furthered the overall resonance of the GJM in society, with the GJM being increasingly recognised as a movement with legitimate criticism and goals. Activists stress that the critique of neoliberal capitalism ceased to be only a niche concern as the movement's ideas started to become increasingly accepted by society. The media are thought to play a central role in this, in particular the end of the initial misrepresentation of the GJM by mainstream media. In contrast to previous events, activists underline how peak events received much more media attention. For example, German activists highlight how after the counter-summit in Genoa, attention 'suddenly exploded' (I12/DE/EP-18). And Italian activists stress how

Genoa 'alphabetised the Italian media because before … nobody spoke about globalisation' (I3/IT/AN-11). In addition, activists emphasise how the event disproved the media's 'apocalypse hysteria', describing activists as 'thugs' (I7/IT/EP-38) and 'terrorists' (I6/PL/AN-24) who have come to demolish the cities of Genoa and Warsaw. 'The reality was exactly the opposite' (I3/IT/AN-11). Especially Polish activists stress with respect to the counter-summit in Warsaw how media coverage of the movement partly improved as 'nothing happened. … We had toilet paper that we threw at them. That was probably the most aggressive moment ever' (I6/PL/AN-7).

Italian activists focus in particular on the counter-summit in Genoa when describing how the GJM challenged the 'pensiero unico' (I1/IT/AN-63) of neoliberalism, how it tore 'apart this curtain [of neoliberalism] to say that "hey, this doesn't work!"'(I19/IT/AC-46). The counter-summit in this vein is described to have expanded the critique of neoliberal globalisation from a minority to a majority, as an activist from a peace group explains:

> Genova changed things. … It showed that … the global justice movement was a culture that was not a minority culture …, and this surprised, this was a shock, and even though the government and the establishment simply tried to portray them as thugs or black blocks or whatever, I think the message [that neoliberal globalisation is problematic] actually got to anyone whose mind was open enough to listen. (I7/IT/EP-38)

German activists similarly emphasise how the GJM challenged neoliberal hegemony by revealing that its promise of 'prosperity, democracy and trickle-down effects … were not kept' (I21/DE/AC-8). Next to Seattle with its 'high political impact with respect to the WTO' (I2/DE/AN-7), German activists particularly regard the counter-summit in Genoa as having increased attention to the problems of neoliberal globalisation and contributed to overcoming neoliberal hegemony in Europe as the following quote illustrates:

> Genoa [was] characterised – on a collective level – by a spirit of optimism, really such a feeling that now something is shifting, this TINA principle, 'there is no alternative' and so forth, it somehow was over. (I24/DE/AC-8)

German activists similarly stress how with the counter-summit in Heiligendamm in 2007 the GJM was 'widely recognised' (I12/DE/EP-63) and the critique of neoliberal globalisation more generally 'found acknowledgement in society' (I23/DE/AC-26) in Germany and beyond.

Also in Poland, activists across sectors hold that particularly the counter-summit in Warsaw in 2004 contributed to the challenge of the neoliberal paradigm. Activists recall how after the 'meaningful event' of the counter-summit in Warsaw (I7/PL/AN-17) perceptions changed with a 'shift in mainstream media discourse' (I3/PL/AN-79). Activists highlight, on the one hand, how the media started portraying the movement more favourably and how journalists realised that 'maybe there is something to it' (I6/PL/AN-44). On the other hand, activists stress that the public opinion about neoliberal capitalism more generally changed after 2004, moving from broad acceptance of neoliberal ideals to a situation where 'people don't believe in it anymore' (I15/PL/AN-8). Similarly, an anarchist activist recalls:

> So around 2004 and the big demonstration in Warsaw, there was I would say a whole ... public sphere shift from the appreciation of capitalism. ... I mean that's incredible but for like 15 years people would believe that .... So there was a whole revision in paradigms. (I18/PL/AC-25)

THE END: DECLINING CROSS-SECTORIAL AND TRANSNATIONAL MOBILISATION

After the peak of the GJM, activists recount a decline in the movement's capacity to mobilise. While activists across countries and sectors associate different events and external triggers with this decline (see chapter 2), they nonetheless attribute similar characteristics to the decline and end of the GJM. This concerns in particular the process of returning back to sector-specific issues and to the local level. This double dispersion is identified as a crucial factor in the GJM's decreasing capacities to mobilise, especially its deteriorating ability to build a broad left movement. In contrast to previous episodes, the GJM loses agency in this last episode as external actors and developments – such as the financial crisis and police repression (see chapter 2) – become more influential again.

Activists' description of this last episode not only differentiates the GJM's declining phase from its peak phase, but also makes a distinction between the GJM and more recent mobilisations. In this way, the description of the GJM's decline and end underlines the GJM's identifying features, namely its powerful broad cross-sectorial coalition and its global approach to neoliberal policies. The more recent protests against austerity and privatisation are considered to largely lack these characteristics. For this reason, they are perceived as a different phase of mobilisation, even though activists identify some continuities with respect to addressed issues, in particular social justice and democratic participation (see chapter 2).

Return to Sectors

Activists associate events after the movement's peak with a considerable decline in cross-sectorial cooperation as each sector 'went back to fight its original enemies'   (I4/IT/AN-10) – for example, trade unions returned to a focus on labour and environmental groups began to again focus more on climate change. Activist describe how after the peak events, differences between left groups became more salient again since conflicts about the forms of protest, organisation and critique re-emerged. Similarly, Italian activists from all sectors recall how after the counter-summit in Genoa an estrangement took place between the different movement sectors with 'some quite serious splits' (I7/IT/EP-39). This is largely attributed to disagreements about repertoires, namely a 'strong dispute ... about violence and non-violence' (I16/IT/AC-16) following the events in Genoa. Also, the failure of the anti-war protests in 2003 is seen to have led to serious divisions (see also chapter 2), as the following statement highlights:

> From this moment [after the anti-war protests], when one understood the incapacity of the movement, which had the maximum size, but didn't have influence in reality, the war continued. ... There was much difficulty to create events with such high participation ...; the relations between the different situations fragmented. (I15/IT/AC-30)

Similarly, German activists describe how divisions between sectors became stronger again after the counter-summit in Heiligendamm in 2007. The movement is considered to have 'branched out' (I22/DE/AC-18), with the broad coalition deteriorating after Heiligendamm. As chapter 2 showed, the reasons for divisions after 2004 are interpreted differently; some stress the 'exhaustion palpable after Heiligendamm' (I23/DE/AC-26), while others highlight the need for new alliances and forms of mobilisation in the context of the financial crisis as it 'changed everything' (I5/DE/AN-15). However, activists across sectors concur that the distance between sectors increased after the counter-summit in Heiligendamm, as 'afterwards ... people were nagging at each other again' (I25/DE/AC-44) and had little understanding for the others' perspectives. An activist from a trade union in this vein describes how the counter-summit was the last time that groups worked together across sectors: 'Heiligendamm was the last grasp [of the GJM], were everyone once again managed to do something together ... but I think this was the last [time]' (I6/DE/AN-36).

Polish activists also identify a decline in cross-sectorial cooperation after the GJM's peak events as groups 'tend to just do things separately' (I17/PL/AC-20), while as described in chapter 2, opinions differ about the timing and causes of the GJM's decline. Anti-neoliberal activists in particular emphasise the deterioration of the ESF after the mid-2000s as well as the divisions within *Attac Poland* after 2003 with which 'began ... a period of ideological conflict' (I1/PL/AN-6). Anti-capitalist activists in contrast stress how in the years following the counter-summit in Warsaw, splits between different radical left groups re-emerged 'really quickly' (I17/PL/AC-10), also within anarchist groups, contributing to the decline of the movement. An anarchist activist concurs and considers these divisions to continue in 2011:

> A lot of really important and really persistent social mobilisation is dispersed right now. ... You see how disintegrated all the different small structures are right now, it's the worst I've seen. (I18/PL/AC-61)

Back to the Local

Along with declining cross-sectorial cooperation, activists describe a 'return to the specific, local critique' (I15/IT/AC-32) towards and after the end of the GJM. Activists elaborate how after the peak of the GJM, activist groups went 'back to the local territories' (I5/IT/AN-6) and how this was connected with addressing more concrete 'everyday' (I20/DE/AC-49) issues. This development is often explained with the limits of the GJM's broad approach – tackling several issues at once – and its 'abstract slogans' (I15/PL/AC-11), especially among Itaian and Polish activists.

Italian activists strongly emphasise how after the peak of the GJM, the movement moved to 'a local territorial scale' (I4/IT/AN-6). This localisation concerns a growing focus on issues in Italy as 'everyone returned to his own country' (I1/IT/AN-10) as well to Italy's different regions. In particular, the campaign against the privatisation of water and the protests against the high-speed train (the 'no TAV' movement) are considered examples of this. This shift to the local also concerns a focus on more concrete issues and forms of criticism: While still connected to the 'global, wide issues that affect us all', activists observe a change from a general critique towards a more local and concrete approach that allows 'targeting the real problems of the people' (I5/IT/AN-6) such as issues of precariousness (see also Zamponi & Daphi, 2014). An activist from a *Centro Sociale* in southern Italy accordingly describes the development:

> And in each territory, experiences were created about the critique of one specific topic, which afterwards was connected to the general topic of the critique. So [now there is] a return: no longer first the general critique and then the local critique, but one starts at the local. (I18/IT/AC-32)

German activists also identify a process of localisation in the context of the GJM's decline. Activists stress how practical solutions were increasingly sought on the local and national levels while still interpreted in the context of the 'interconnectedness' (FG/DE/AC-114) of neoliberal globalisation. The more abstract form of critique of the global approach is regarded as less problematic overall than in Italy and Poland. Partly, the development towards more local organising is considered to have already started before the counter-summit in Heiligendamm. Anti-neoliberal activists in this context for example highlight the protests against changes in social policy in Germany from 2004 onwards (see chapter 2) as well as *Attac's* growing local chapters. Anti-capitalist activists in this respect stress in particular the focus on more concrete local issues in the recent protests against austerity as well as the 'locally concretised' Arab Spring (I23/DE/AC-32). An activist from *Attac* concurs:

> [After Genoa] the movement localised, that is no longer primarily meeting and developing in global summits, but started to ... form and act more on the country and local levels, in cities and so forth. I would call the period after Genoa a period of localisation of the global justice movement, at least in Europe. (I5/ DE/AN-13)

Similarly, Polish activists describe how activism localised after the GJM's peak. Activists describe how after the mid-2000s, mobilisation changed from 'protesting against the big system' (I17/PL/AC-26) to addressing more local and concrete issues close to 'Polish reality' (I2/PL/AN-4). In particular, the tenants' movement is considered an example of this development (see chapter 2). Such processes of localisation are often connected to a critique of the 'alterglobalist tourism' (I20/PL/AC-18) of transnational protest events being 'just a hobby ... not social work' since 'you do not work with ordinary people, with people who are oppressed, who are thrown out of work, who need help' (I16/PL/AC-11). The following quote outlines this localisation of protests in Poland:

> At some point ... a lot of people were like 'think globally' and protest ... at the G8 ... when actually they should be doing something in their area. ... But right now let's say that it's, in Poland for sure it's becoming more local, ... people would read about it ... and they know what issues we're talking about because we're talking about the issues of their everyday life ... yeah, that changed. (I17/ PL/AC-26)

CONCLUSION

This chapter explored shared patterns in stories that activists tell about the GJM. It showed that along with country- and sector-specific patterns with respect to the events and actors that activists consider to be primary, they also share a broad 'GJM narrative' across countries and sectors. In particular, I illuminated how activists order the different GJM events and experiences into a shared plot with a sequence of four episodes. Each episode does not necessarily contain the same events, but activists ascribe common characteristics to each episode across countries and sectors. In this way, the GJM narrative integrates the country- and sector-specific GJM experiences without negating differences. Against the background of the considerable differences in the composition, scale and timing of GJM mobilisations in each country (see the Introduction chapter), it is remarkable how clearly and consistently activists distinguish between these different phases of the GJM's development across countries as well as sectors.

The Shared Plot

I have first shown how activists across countries and sectors contrast the GJM with a prior situation in which the left is presented as weak and divided and in which neoliberalism is seen to dominate society and politics. Such a contrast tends to exaggerate the weaknesses of the left and to neglect mobilisations prior to the GJM. This highlights the GJM's novelty and its noteworthy characteristics, in particular its ability to build broad coalitions across the left and its capacity to challenge the hegemony of neoliberalism. This emphasis on differences from prior mobilisations has also been observed in other movements and serves to underline the noteworthiness and legitimacy of a present movement (e.g., Polletta, 1998b, 2006; Flesher Fominaya, 2015; Armstrong & Crage, 2006). Cristina Flesher Fominaya (2015), for example, describes the 'strategic amnesia' of Spanish Indignados activists with respect to deliberative democratic practices already used in the context of the GJM. And as discussed in chapter 1, Francesca Polletta (1998b, 2006) observes with respect to U.S. student sit-ins in the 1960s how activists emphasised their own spontaneity to distinguish themselves from the gradualism and hierarchy of previous Black movements. While the drawn contrast is similar, the content of differences varies in the present case: while the differences identified in the case of the GJM concern broad left coalitions and the challenge of neoliberal hegemony, in the case of the Spanish Indignados the differences concerns deliberative democratic practices and in the U.S. student sit-ins they concern the immediacy and organisation of activism.

The shared plot I have identified above additionally goes beyond such initial contrasting as it also entails a clear turning point and a build-up episode that prepares the peak of the GJM. In this way, I have shown how activists identify build-up events as important first steps in mobilising against neoliberal globalisation in their narratives and how they differentiate these events from later peak events. Build-up events, while presented as offering first successes in terms of political impact (such as stopping trade deals in the case of the campaign against the MAI agreement) as well as in developing transnational activist ties and horizontal organisation, are centrally associated with failures and disappointments. The GJM in this episode is described to have yet not developed its full potential as left divisions continued and the public resonance to protests against anti-neoliberalism was low or negative as neoliberal hegemony remained largely intact. Such stress on initial failures and limited successes not only highlights the GJM's later successes, it also delineates a process of collective learning.

In activists' narratives this situation is reported to have changed considerably in the context of peak events. Activists describe peak events as turning points that reversed the prior situation, both with respect to the hegemony of neoliberalism and the divisions within the left as well as regarding the GJM's limited success in the beginning. Both obstacles are considered to have been overcome in peak events thanks to strong cross-sectorial cooperation and positive public responses. The GJM here is thought to have reached its full potential, developing a strong agency. Hence, in contrast to the various disappointments associated with the build-up events, activists underline the peak's successes with an emphasis on shared feelings of joy, pride and triumph. Along with the different degrees of success in the build-up and peak episodes, I have also revealed that these episodes are associated with different kinds of successes: events of the build-up episode are much more prominently associated with successes in building transnational cooperation, peak events more with successes in building cross-sectorial cooperation. This difference points to the fact that activists prioritise GJM achievements: since primarily associated with peak events, achievements in cross-sectorial cooperation seem to be defined as the greater challenge and success of the GJM. In defining transnational cooperation as the central achievement of build-up rather than peak events, achievements in this area seem to be considered less problematic and as a precondition for building cross-sectorial solidarity (see also Daphi, 2014b).

Finally, I have shown how activists cluster together GJM events after the peak in a last episode that delineates the GJM's decline and end. Events in this episode are characterised by the decreasing capacity to mobilise across sectors and countries. Activists on the one hand describe a 'return to sectors' as disagreements between the different groups became more salient again and splits reoccurred. On the other hand, they observe processes of 'localisation' as activism started focusing more on issues in the own countries and regions and on growingly concrete issues. This description not only draws a distinction between the peak events and those of decline, but also a distinction between the GJM and later movements. Activists accordingly consider that mobilisations from the late 2000s onwards lack the GJM's ability to mobilise transnationally and build broad left coalitions.

Defining the GJM

The 'GJM narrative' constitutes a story of collective conversion that bridges the different national and sectorial perspectives on the GJM through the four shared episodes: the situation prior to the GJM, the GJM's build-up, its peak and end. Different sectorial, national and transnational events in this way are woven into a coherent plot defining a beginning, a turning point and an end. This plot constructs a sense of shared experience that allows activists to make sense of the various events and actors over the years as part of a joint movement. This sense of shared experience underlines commonalities within the GJM with respect to shared cognitions, boundaries and emotional proximity. In particular, the shared success in challenging neoliberal hegemony and overcoming divisions within the left played a primary role here.

First, the joint experience in challenging neoliberal hegemony underlines the GJM's *shared cognitions* about goals and problems with respect to the joint master frame of anti-neoliberalism. The first three shared episodes clearly outline the opposition to neoliberalism as the central problem that needs to be addressed – from elaborations of its omnipresence and detrimental effects on society in the first episode, to limited first attempts in challenging it in the build-up episode and to the successes in mobilising a broad and publicly visible movement against it in the peak episode. This shows more generally how shared cognitions about goals and problems need not necessarily be stated explicitly ('we want …'), but can also be formulated more implicitly in narratives, for example, in telling a story about the negative repercussions of neoliberal policies.

Second, the joint experience in challenging neoliberal hegemony as well as in building a broad left network draw clear *social boundaries*, delineating the GJM vis-à-vis other actors. This concerns two sets of boundaries: on the one hand, the GJM narrative draws boundaries between the GJM and agents advocating and promoting neoliberal globalisation; on the other hand between the GJM and previous and later social movements which activists consider as less successful in challenging neoliberal policies (in particular movements prior to the GJM) and also less successful in building a broad left coalition (both before and after the GJM). Through such a contrast, activists delineate the GJM as a distinctive actor, despite the diversity of national constellations of mobilisation and sectorial perspectives and the GJM's overall open and tolerant approach (della Porta, 2005a; Daro, 2009; Daphi, 2014b).

Finally, both the experiences in challenging neoliberal hegemony as well as in building a broad left network provide a sense of shared hardship and triumph of GJM activists across countries and sectors that strengthens and expresses *emotional proximity*. Experiences of hardship in particular concern the shared frustration and disappointment that activists report in the first and second episodes with respect to the omnipresence of neoliberal thinking and the divisions within the left and the difficulties this posed for left mobilisation and positive public resonance. Activists highlight experiences of triumph in the context of peak events particularly with references to the shared joy and pride felt when being able to mobilise despite the aforementioned obstacles. Such positive and shared feelings are especially connected to the growing public resonance of the movement in connection with disproving the misrepresentation of GJM activists as terrorists and thugs as well as to the success in building a broad left coalition.

NOTE

1. In addition to sector-specific events such as the first World Social Forum (WSF) in the case of anti-neoliberal activists and the counter-summit in Prague in the case of anti-capitalist activists (see details in chapter 2).

Chapter 4

The GJM Narrative
and Movement Identity

As the links grew, more stories were added to the flow, accounts of audacity and courage, moments of magic and hope. ... Layer upon layer of stories travelled along the thin copper threads of the internet, strengthening the global network and developing relationships between diverse groups and individuals. (Doc11-INT, p. 65)

How important is telling a particular story about the GJM to building and maintaining movement identity? As the previous chapter showed, activists share a specific 'GJM narrative' across sectors and countries which delineates the GJM's shared frames, boundaries and emotional proximity. This chapter will underline the connection between this shared narrative and GJM identity by showing that the GJM narrative is shared only by activists who feel like part of the movement at large. The GJM narrative hence is specific to a particular group at a particular period of time. It has been developed and maintained by GJM activists over many years until the point when other engagements became more salient, that is, when activists no longer felt like part of the movement and ceased to be involved or became involved in a new cycle of mobilisation. The GJM narrative hence seems to have played a central role in forming and maintaining GJM identity.

Below, I will first show that GJM activists had shared central elements of the GJM narrative for several years by drawing on a comparison between my interviews conducted in 2011 and 2012 and central GJM publications between 1997 and 2005. In the second part I will demonstrate that the GJM narrative identified in chapter 3 is specific to activists who feel like part of the GJM. Activists primarily considering themselves part of specific GJM groups recount the GJM in a different way, as do activists who no longer feel part of the GJM in 2011 and 2012 or in 2015. Central characteristics of the shared

GJM narrative in these cases are missing, highlighting how closely connected this narrative is with sharing GJM identity.

This chapter combines the narrative interviews with GJM activists analysed in the previous chapters with other data. The first part compares narrative patterns in activists interviews from 2011/2012 identified in chapter 3 with central GJM publications from the movement's early years. These publications allow insights into early stories activists tell about the GJM.[1] The publications cover the different GJM sectors and a time period in which central GJM events took place in the Italian, German and Polish GJM (see appendix B): in Italy the time frame covered ranges from shortly before the counter-summit in Genoa to the first European Social Forum in Florence (2000–2002), in Germany from shortly before the counter-summit in Cologne to the anti-war demonstrations (1998–2003) and in Poland from the counter-summit in Prague to shortly after the counter-summit in Warsaw (2000–2005). In addition, a number of international publications have been included in the analysis between 1997 and 2004 to illuminate also the transnational discursive context (see appendix B). The second part of this chapter compares the interviews analysed in the previous chapters (with activists who feel like part of the GJM at large) with interviews conducted in the same years with activists either no longer identifying with the GJM or primarily identifying with specific GJM groups, as well as with follow-up interviews conducted with Italian activists in 2015.

CONTINUITY OF THE GJM NARRATIVE FROM 1997 TO 2012

As the literature on collective memory emphasises, memories are always shaped by present conditions. Accordingly, narratives about the GJM can be expected to change as the political and social contexts of mobilisation vary over time. However, a comparison of activists' narratives in 2011 and 2012 with those in early GJM publications of different sectors (see details in appendix B) shows that narratives are remarkably similar. From early on, activists share central elements of the 'GJM narrative' identified in chapter 3. These concern in particular the clear boundary drawn between previous mobilisations and the turning point identified with respect to overcoming left divides and neoliberal hegemony (see chapter 3). Of course some elements also are different; first, events in each episode changed over time. Furthermore, in particular the end of the story is more open in early publications as mobilisation was still in full flow at that time. Also, build-up events in terms of lessons learned along the way are reported in less detail. However, activists already in the early GJM years order the GJM events into similar episodes as later on, clearly distinguishing peak events from earlier ones with respect to their success in overcoming left divides and neoliberal hegemony. This shows how the GJM narrative has been developed and maintained over several years, linking specific sectorial and national experiences into a shared framework.

Prior to Us a Desert: Weaknesses of the Left and Neoliberal Hegemony

Already in early GJM publications, activists draw a clear distinction between the GJM and the situation prior to the GJM. As in 2011 and 2012, they contrast the GJM in particular with the prior dearth of action with respect to the defeat of the left and the dominance of neoliberal thought and practice. In this vein, in international GJM publications, the notion of the 'defeat and disorientation of the left' is prominent from early on, connected to the 'end of history' with the collapse of the Soviet Union (Doc13-INT, p. 21) and the growing 'totalitarianism of the market' (Doc2-INT, p. 121). This situation is juxtaposed with the GJM's strength constituting 'a true international' (Doc7-INT, para. 7), as also noted in an international collection of reports about direct actions of grassroots GJM groups:

> At the time, the Zapatista uprising seemed to come from out of nowhere. The 1990s was a time of triumphant optimism for capitalism. The old enemy of the Soviet Empire had collapsed, and with it the remaining opposition to the capitalist system. Economic globalisation – the imposition of the 'free' market into every corner of the globe – was worshipped by economists as a kind of fundamentalist religion. (Doc10-INT, p. 22)

Italian activists similarly stress in early publications that with the 'crisis of real socialism' (Doc11-IT, p. 9) 'the patrons of globalisation are as powerful as never before in human history' (Doc8-IT, p. 204).[2] And as 'everything is subordinated to the *pensiero unico* of profit' this leaves no 'space for critical thinking and for social needs' (Doc4-IT, 2001, p. 38). Very similar to my interviews in 2011, Italian activists in these early publications juxtapose the GJM with 'failures' (Doc11-IT, p. 9) and 'strained relations' (Doc1-IT, 2000, para. 16) of the left in previous decades, in particular the 'defeat of the 70s' (Doc5-IT, para. 16). The GJM in this vein is described as 'a new generation of resistance' (Doc14-IT, p. 1) because of its focus on 'global issues' (Doc3-IT, p. 14) and its 'convergence in diversity' (Doc15-IT, p. 5). An anti-neoliberal Italian activist concurs:

> What happened in Genoa does not have precedents in the second half of the 20th century. It's useless to try to bring it together ... with the 60s, the 68, the 77. There is nothing to see. It's a different thing, qualitatively as well as quantitatively. (Doc8-IT, p. 206)

German activists also stress the dominance of the new 'comprehensive economic order' (Doc2-DE, p. 4) in early publications and connect it to the 'long depression of movements' (Doc10-DE, p. 3), especially since the collapse of the Soviet Union. As in the interviews in 2011 and 2012, activists highlight how mobilisations in the 1980s and 1990s remained considerably 'isolated' (Doc5-DE, para. 3) and lacked a transnational dimension in contrast to the later 'globalisation of protest' (Doc8-DE, p. 1). An activist from a Trotskyist group shares this sentiment:

> After the collapse of the Stalinist states between '89 and '91, capitalism entered a phase of euphoria. A new world order was proclaimed that was supposed to bring peace and prosperity. ... Socialists who continued to point to capitalism's proneness to crisis and the growing social inequalities for years sounded like priests in the desert. (Doc7-DE, p. 3)

Similarly, Polish activists in early publications stress the 'triumph' of neoliberal capitalism after the 'collapse of the Eastern bloc' (Doc9-PL, para. 1) and its 'ever-insatiable hunger for profits' (Doc11-PL, para. 22). The 'new world economic order' is described to have crucially shaped Polish transformation, its 'thugs in suits' increasing inequality and poverty in Poland and elsewhere (Doc2-PL, para. 29). This situation is considered to have considerably weakened the left, wasting 'the whole human potential of that era' (Doc5-PL, para. 12) and is contrasted with the GJM and its 'global' mobilisation of the left (Doc10-PL, para. 16). An anarchist activist agrees:

> The weakness of the critical movement is hardly a fault of the critics themselves. The responsibility for neoliberalism's unflagging rhetoric of success ... lies primarily with the agents of neoliberalism and neo-conservatism [and] the official media's unabated tone reminiscent of the Margaret Thatcher era – TINA, TINA, TINA. ... The vastness of the free market propaganda is visible at first glance, because any questioning of the current shape of the economy, or society meets with reactions as if one doubts the roundness of the earth. (Doc1-PL, para.18)

Overcoming Divisions in the Left and Neoliberal Hegemony

Furthermore, the GJM publications show that activists already in early years identify peaks of mobilisation with characteristics similar to activists' narratives in 2011 and 2012. As in 2011 and 2012, activists in early publications associate peak events with the GJM's ability to overcome left divides and successfully challenge neoliberal hegemony. Such successful challenge similarly is connected to the growing overall resonance of the GJM and to defying the initial disregard and misrepresentation in the media (see chapter 3), especially in Italian and Polish publications. Of course, since GJM mobilisations were still in full flow at that time, successes in these areas tend to be more often combined with debates about how to proceed and what to improve than in the interviews I conducted in 2011 and 2012. Nonetheless, certain events are described as turning points in this respect, including GJM protests and events in the late 1990s. In international GJM publications, for example, various early GJM events are described as successes in challenging neoliberal globalisation and building a broad coalition, bringing together 'unionists … "anti-globalists," unemployed, *Attac*, progressive parties and the left' (Doc3-INT, para. 1). Activists describe, for example, how the protests against the WTO in Geneva in 1998 'at one stroke transformed the WTO from an unknown acronym to a very controversial institution with a very bad public image' (Doc1-INT, para. 8). In particular, the counter-summit in Seattle, the following 'global confrontations' and the first World Social Forums in Porto Alegre are described as capable of 'strip[ping] down' the empire and to make it 'drop its mask' (Doc14-INT, p. 53), becoming 'a very real threat to global capitalism' (Doc12-INT, p. 14) by 'discredit[ing] the institutions of globalisation' (Doc6-INT, p. 4). Successes in 'sowing unrest among the dignitaries of the institutions' (Doc4-INT, p. 5) and in shutting down summits of international organisations accordingly are identified with respect to various protests after Seattle. Next to the counter-summit in Genoa in 2001, for example, the counter-summits in Nice in 2000 (e.g., Doc3-INT) and in Barcelona in 2002 (e.g., Doc5-INT), are described in this way. The following statement from Susan George, then vice-president of *Attac France*, shows this understanding:

We are no longer on the defensive. This movement has already changed the framework and the themes of the debate. We have forced the responsible bodies to take our arguments seriously. Neoliberalism is no longer the dominant religion in the world for the simple reason that it does not work. (Doc8-INT, p. 142)

Similarly, activists in Italy stress in early publications that 'events from Seattle onwards were very useful to undermine the liberal ideological hegemony' (Doc18-IT, p. 6). These publications furthermore highlight successes in building a broad coalition with 'many cultures, many actors involved' (Doc15-IT, p. 5) in a 'rich blend of content and form' (Doc17-IT, p. 2), as activists were able to identify 'a point of commonality in the struggles' (Doc1-IT, para. 17). Such achievements are linked to various events. For example, the 'failure of Seattle in the face of unprecedented protest' (Doc6-IT, p. 1) is highlighted and described to confirm 'a new movement which had regained civil society's participation' (Doc2-IT, para. 17). Similarly, especially anti-capitalist activists describe the early end of the IMF and World Bank summit in Prague in 2000 as a success of 'the validity of a new way of finding ourselves side by side in the world's streets, confronting global problems' (Doc1-IT, para. 12). Across sectors, activists highlight in particular the counter-summit in Genoa as a success in challenging neoliberal globalisation. The repression during the protests in Genoa is regarded as a sign of weakness of the 'powerful' being afraid 'that the Seattle worm had dug so deep to shake the rock-solid consensus they need' (Doc13-IT, p. 4). In addition, 'the fierce repression suffered in Genoa' (Doc7-IT, p. 3) is described as a challenge that the GJM successfully mastered owing to its ability to stay together during the counter-summit in Genoa as well as after it.[3] Especially anti-neoliberal and eco-pacifist activists furthermore stress that the ESF in Florence in 2002 demonstrated the 'maturity' of the GJM in jointly defying the media misrepresentation since 'everything took place without incident, not even an ingrown toenail' (Doc16-IT, p. 2). *Attac* activists in this vein underline the GJM's capacity to challenge neoliberal hegemony in 2001 in relation to Seattle:

> This connection between different cultures and experiences, capable of overcoming the illusion of self-sufficiency and self-reference, has produced a collective with the potential to produce a cultural hegemony to confront the crisis of the paradigm of the *pensiero unico* of the market, and the strategic failures of the social democratic hypothesis. (Doc9-IT, p. 216)

German activists also stress turning points in overcoming left divides and challenging neoliberal globalisation in early publications. The GJM's peak events are accordingly considered central in creating legitimacy problems for neoliberals' 'unscrupulous gambling' (Doc3-DE, p. 17) and in maintaining and extending the GJM's broad coalition 'affirming plurality' (Doc11-DE, p. 60). The earliest publications in particular stress the achievements of the counter-summit in Seattle. With the failure of official negotiations ending 'without a tangible outcome' (Doc1-DE, para. 1), the GJM's protests became 'impossible to ignore' (Doc4-DE, para. 5). The summit's failure and the GJM's success is also associated with repression as those in charge in Seattle were 'only able to cope with the resistance' by declaring a 'state of emergency' (Doc2-DE, p. 5). German *Attac* activists concur in an editorial of their newsletter *Sand im Getriebe*:

> Who would have thought: the GJM is making world history. What started in Seattle, transformed into a veritable worldwide movement, into a second globalisation, a globalisation of protest against the two big evils of our time: the neoliberal offensive and imperial war. (Doc8-DE, p. 1)

In later German publications the counter-summit in Seattle, however, plays a less prominent role so that the successes of Seattle overall are less central in these publications than in my interviews in 2011 and 2012. Later publications especially consider the counter-summit in Genoa, the ESF in Florence and the demonstrations against the war in Iraq as crucial in deepening the legitimacy crisis of neoliberal globalisation with the 'powers against war and neoliberalism growing stronger' and with the GJM 'broadening its political base' (Doc9-DE, p. 16). The counter-summit in Genoa is in this way described as unprecedented in its 'quality, unity and its radical content' (Doc6-DE, para. 44).

Polish activists in early publications similarly stress the ability of the GJM to overcome left divides and neoliberal hegemony with 'a real impact on global politics' (Doc5-PL, para. 61). Already by this time, activists consider various early GJM events successful in bringing together various groups and 'undermining' neoliberal globalisation's institutions, for example, with respect to 'the role of the IMF, WB' (Doc7-PL, para. 42). The protests against the MAI agreement in 1998, for example, are stressed to have effectively 'overthrown' the 'secret agreement' (Doc10-PL, para. 14; also Doc2-PL). And the WTO negotiations in Seattle in 1999 are described to have 'ended in failure and disgrace ... thanks to the joint action of 1,600 organisations worldwide' (Doc6-PL, para. 4). However, it is particularly events from the counter-summit in Genoa onwards that are considered to have more fully brought capitalism and its 'fanatical transformation of all areas ... into profit' (Doc4-PL, para. 33) 'onto the defensive' (Doc9-PL, para. 1). In this context, activists, for example, contrast the counter-summit in Prague in 2000 with the counter-summit in Genoa in 2001 and the ESF in Florence in 2002. While the counter-summit in Prague is considered to be largely defeated by the media's 'psychosis of fear' (Doc3-PL, para. 2), activists highlight that 'protesters achieved a total propaganda victory' in Genoa as well as during the ESF in Florence. This victory is largely attributed to the unprecedented number of people coming together 'contesting the current economic and social system' and especially owing to the ESF's 'peaceful atmosphere' (Doc8-PL, para. 22). An *Attac* activist shares this sentiment:

> Protests against the G8 summit in Genoa represent a turning point in the history of social anti-globalism.[4] 300,000 people took to the streets of the Italian city. ... It was supposed to be an apocalypse. ... And this event best reflects the gap between what the Italian government and the press threatened and what actually happened in Genoa. ... Genoa is an important step towards creating an alternative to the world of the rich oligarchs. ... Next to the mass mobilisation Genoa has also shown the ability to create alternatives to liberal globalisation. (Doc3-PL, para. 1–14)

The counter-summit in Warsaw in 2004 is described to continue this development, illustrating how 'the movement for global justice grows and gains new, politically awakened heart' (Doc11-PL, para. 22).

THE LIMITS OF THE GJM NARRATIVE: GROUP-SPECIFIC AND DETACHED NARRATIVES

The 'GJM narrative' discussed above and in chapter 3 is not shared by everyone; it is specific to a certain group of activists at a particular point in time. Only activists considering themselves part of the GJM at large share this narrative. Others tell the GJM story differently. This concerns 'group activists' who feel primarily part of a certain group rather than the GJM at large in 2011/2012 as well as 'detached activists' who no longer feel part of the GJM in 2011/2012 as well as in 2015.[5] These activists' narratives miss central characteristics of the GJM narrative described in chapter 3, in particular the clear boundaries drawn between previous and later movements as well as the identification of a turning point in terms of GJM successes (compare chapter 3). Group-specific narratives lack GJM boundaries and turning points due to the focus on group-specific developments, while narratives by activists no longer identifying with the GJM lack boundaries and turning points overall due to doubts about the GJM's impact.

Group-Specific Narratives

Activists who primarily feel like part of certain groups within the GJM rather than the GJM at large[6] tend to not share central elements of the GJM narrative. In particular, two characteristics are missing. First, they de-emphasise the differences between previous and later mobilisations. Second, build-up and peak events are not understood as a concern of the GJM and its challenge of overcoming left divisions and neoliberal hegemony, but rather as an issue of group-specific goals and challenges. Of course, also activists considering themselves part of the larger GJM recount group-specific events (see sector-specific differences in chapter 2), however, in contrast to activists primarily identifying with a specific group, they *combine* sector-specific events and developments with the GJM's broader development. In this way, activists primarily identifying with a specific group tell group or sector-specific narratives that do not delineate shared experiences of the GJM at large but those of a specific group or sector.

Missing Boundaries: Continuity with Previous and Later Mobilisations

Activists who were involved in GJM mobilisations but define themselves primarily as part of a particular group emphasise the continuity in mobilisations prior to and after the GJM's main phase. Continuities in particular are identified with respect to mobilisations that are close to activists' own groups in terms of addressed issues, tactics or form of organisation. The boundaries of the GJM, as a specific wave of mobilisation, in these narratives are hence more blurred than in narratives by activists considering themselves part of the GJM at large.

In this way, 'group activists' highlight similarities rather than differences between the GJM and previous mobilisations, defining the latter as crucial lead-ups to the GJM or even as part of it. In particular, continuities with respect to addressed issues and the degree of international cooperation are stressed. For example, activists in Italy and Germany who are linked to international solidarity movements – both from anti-capitalist and from eco-pacifist sectors – stress that the GJM 'started long before the 90s' (I18/DE/AC-8) with liberation movements against (neo-)colonial rule and related international solidarity mobilisations; for instance, with respect to Nicaragua in the 1970s (I18/DE/AC, I16/DE/EP). Addressing colonial legacies and imperialism in this context 'was not yet called [the] Global Justice Movement but content wise on this line' (I16/DE/EP-2).

Furthermore, 'group activists' from environmental groups in Italy and Germany stress, for example, that environmental movements from the 1980s onwards were central predecessors of the GJM because they had been raising concerns with neoliberal globalisation (I15/DE/EP, I14/IT/EP). An Italian environmental activist in this context traces the beginnings of the GJM to the movement against nuclear power in Italy and Europe because it was a 'vanguard' in linking issues of justice with environmental protection (I14/IT/EP-3).

In other examples from Poland, anti-neoliberal 'group activists' emphasise continuities with the *Solidarność* movement in the 1980s and its broad struggle for social justice. In this vein, an *Attac* activist describes the left wing of the *Solidarność* movement as 'proto-alterglobalist' (I11/PL/AN-4).

'Group activists' additionally emphasise similarities rather than differences between the GJM and later mobilisations in contrast to activists who feel part of the GJM at large (see chapter 3). Group activists hence tend to argue that the GJM continued in 2011 and 2012. Though also group activists largely regard the GJM as weakened and 'extremely diversified' (I16/DE/EP-23), in some sectors these activists consider GJM activism to continue or even intensify, particularly if areas of activism are concerned to which activists feel close. In this vein, for example, 'group activists' from environmental groups in Italy and Germany stress the continuity of the GJM's quest for social justice in the context of the intensifying mobilisation for climate justice starting in 2007, since 'economy, work and health … all have to do with climate change' (I14/IT/EP-29). An environmental activist from Germany similarly stresses the continuity of activist gatherings for climate issues such as the McPlanet (2003–2012) meetings in Germany and the international Degrowth Conferences (2008–) (I15/DE/EP).

'Group activists' connected to *Attac* and other anti-neoliberal groups in Germany and Poland similarly stress that mobilisations against neoliberal policies and international institutions continue and grow stronger in the context of the financial crisis from 2007 onwards, in particular with respect to issues of work and social security. Activists especially highlight the role of their own group in this continued mobilisation, for example, *Attac* (I11/ PL/AN, I3/DE/AN), the Polish publishing project and think tank *Krytyka Polityczna* (I9/PL/AN) or the German trade union *IG-Metall* (I7/DE/AN). The Occupy and Indignados movements in this vein are described as a 'deja-vu' because of similarities with GJM protests around 2000 (I3/DE/AN-14) and even with the struggles '30 years ago' in the context of the *Solidarność* movement in Poland (I11/PL/AN-11). Moreover, anti-capitalist and eco-pacifist activists in Italy and Germany connected to international solidar-ity movements similarly stress the continuity of mobilisations around the inequalities between the so-called Global North and Global South. An activist from an international aid organisation in this context highlights that mobilisa-tion continues in Italy as 'you cannot simply end the critique of a model of development' (I12/IT/EP-25), and a German internationalist activist similarly elaborates how 'postcolonial learning continues' (I17/DE/AC-23).

Common Experiences Missing: Group-Specific Turning Points

Like the 'GJM narrative' identified in chapter 3, narratives by activists primar-ily considering themselves part of a particular group largely identify a turning point in their narratives in which a previous situation is overcome. However, unlike the GJM narrative, transformation processes in group narratives do not concentrate on overcoming left divides and neoliberal hegemony. Instead, turning points in these narratives concern overcoming group- or sector-spe-cific challenges. Hence, the common thread of group narratives is the develop-ment of the activists' own group or sector, rather than the development of the GJM at large. For example, narratives by *Attac* 'group activists' in Poland and Germany focus on the development of *Attac* and the challenges it mastered. In this vein, achievements of *Attac* rather than the overall challenge of over-coming divides in the left and neoliberal hegemony constitute the peak events in these narratives: in Poland the foundation of *Attac* in 2001 and the Polish Social Forum organised in 2010 (I11/PL/AN) and in Germany the significant growth of *Attac* after the counter-summit in Genoa (I3/DE/AN).

Similarly, 'group activists' in Germany and Poland connected to unions or syndicalist groups focus their narratives on struggles around labour, and identify turning points in the context of their group. For example, a Ger-man union activist concentrates his narrative of the growing cooperation of unions with social movements, culminating in joint mobilisations against falling social standards from the mid-2000s onwards (I7/DE/AN). A Polish activist from an anarcho-syndicalist group likewise considers the change from a more global critique 'emphasising globalisation' to addressing social issues and work in Poland after 2004 to be the central turning point (I21/PL/AC-19). Environmental activists in Italy and Germany similarly focus their turning points on successfully linking the issues of social justice with environmental justice: initially, mainly environmental groups are described to have understood that 'unjust trade relations' are connected to environmental damage (I15/DE/EP-2). In the course of GJM mobilisations, this situation is considered to have transformed as the insight that environmental destruction and social injustice are linked became widely shared (I15/DE/EP, I14/IT/EP).

Furthermore, anti-capitalist and eco-pacifist 'group activists' in Italy and Germany connected to international solidarity movements focus their stories on the growing cooperation between the Global North and South and identify turning points related to this cooperation (I16/DE/EP, I12+I13/IT/EP, I17+18/DE/AC). The concern of anti-capitalist activists is in particular the growth of 'new internationalism' inspired by the Zapatistas, that is, the connection of struggles against inequality in different parts of the world instead of 'helping' struggles in the Global South. Turning points accordingly concern the foundation and growth of groups in this area, for example, the foundation of *Peoples' Global Action* (PGA) in 1998 (I17+I18/DE/AC).

Detached Narratives: Missing GJM Agency

Activists who no longer feel like part of the GJM tell a different story than activists who still do. This concerns both activists no longer considering themselves part of the GJM in the interviews in 2011 and 2012 as well as in follow-up interviews in 2015. Central elements of the 'GJM narrative' identified in chapter 3 are no longer shared in these cases. In particular, these narratives miss a clearly defined peak. Either a turning point is missing altogether as central events are not considered effective in overcoming left divides or challenging neoliberal globalisation (activists who no longer feel like part of the movement in 2011 and 2012), or such achievements are attributed to external events rather than the power of the GJM (follow-up interviews in 2015). These narratives hence de-emphasise the GJM's capacity to change the status quo and its agency. In addition, similar to the group-specific narratives, boundaries drawn to earlier and later movements are less distinct in these narratives.

No Longer Part of the GJM in 2011 and 2012

Some of the activists interviewed in 2011 and 2012 no longer consider themselves part of the GJM.[7] These 'detached activists' tend to tell narratives about the GJM that lack a peak. They identify overcoming left divides and neoliberal hegemony as the central challenges of the GJM – similar to activists still considering themselves part of the GJM in 2011 and 2012 (and different from the 'group activists'). However, these goals are not considered achieved as the GJM is described to have failed to overcome left divisions and neoliberal hegemony. Accordingly, problems of the GJM in mobilising a broad coalition and in convincing the public of its proposals are more emphasised in these narratives than in others.

'Detached activists' tend to move from recounting build-up events – the growing critique of neoliberal globalisation and the attempts to build a broad movement – directly to a description of the GJM's decline or its limited vigour. In particular, the GJM's limited capacity for bringing together different sectors and countering the dominance of neoliberal thinking are highlighted in this context. For example, a German eco-pacifist activist describes the dynamics in building up the movement in the late 1990s and early 2000s based on the shared goal of preventing the 'catastrophe' of neoliberal globalisation, but she goes on to stress that solutions to this problem were very different and difficult to bridge (I14/DE/EP-7) without recounting large protest events or achievements. In a publication in 2001, the same activist in contrast very clearly highlights the success of Seattle in triggering the 'failure' of negotiations as well as kicking off the ensuing growth of the movement culminating in Genoa with the 'largest political protest' to date.[8]

Similarly, an Italian anti-neoliberal activist describes the openness towards new political cultures in the early 1990s connected to the Zapatista uprising and Seattle, but he continues his narrative by emphasising how the different perspectives never really merged in the GJM. The anti-war demonstrations in this vein are described to show 'how you didn't really achieve anything' with respect to the economic and political crises (I6/IT/AN-19). Likewise, Polish anti-neoliberal activists no longer identifying with the GJM emphasise how little impact the counter-summit in Warsaw had as it was largely a 'shallow' protest in which people 'just babble' (I5/PL/AN-45), a mere 'media event' (I8/PL/AN-15) that revealed that large and enduring mobilisation was not achieved.

Furthermore, boundaries to previous and later mobilisations are less pronounced in narratives by 'detached activists'. Activists either do not mention differences from the left 'desert' previous to the GJM or highlight certain continuities. For example, an Italian anti-neoliberal activist highlights how the move away from twentieth-century political institutions in the early 1990s draws on ideas from movements of the 1960s and 1970s (I6/IT/AN). A Polish anti-neoliberal activist similarly stresses the maturity of social movements critical of neoliberal transformation in the early 1990s, arguing 'it's not like that that once upon a time some guys in Seattle started to make a demonstration in the streets and then it went "snap"' (I5/PL/AN-8).

In addition, continuities with later mobilisations are stressed. Rather than identifying the GJM as a distinct phase of mobilisation, 'detached activists' tend to describe the struggle for social justice as ongoing despite being 'very weak' (I6/IT/AN-22) and 'running out of steam' (I8/PL/AN-17). The struggle for social justice in this vein is described as 'something that accumulates' because of the continuation of addressed topics (I6/IT/AN-22) and 'established networks' (I4/DE/AN-14).

Activists in 2015

Follow-up interviews in 2015 with Italian activists interviewed already in 2011[9] show that while activists shared all elements of the 'GJM narrative' in 2011, four years later with a new phase of mobilisation maturing, activists' stories change. Similar to the activists who no longer felt part of the GJM in 2011 and 2012, activists' narratives in 2015 are less distinct with respect to identifying a turning point and drawing boundaries to previous and later movements. In particular, activists ascribe successes of the GJM to external factors rather than to the strength of the movement and hence attribute less agency to the GJM.

In this way, activists tend to emphasise the overall success of the GJM less in the follow-up interviews in 2015 than in those conducted in 2011. Between 2011 and 2015, enthusiasm about the GJM's peak events and its diverse crowd seem to be decreasing. Particularly striking here is that in 2015 achievements in overcoming left divisions and neoliberal hegemony are less attributed to the GJM's mobilisation capacity and more to external events. For instance, an eco-pacifist activist in 2015 emphasises the role of the Internet in building and maintaining the GJM's global ties and mobilisation (I9b/IT/EP), while in 2011 this factor was hardly mentioned and the GJM's achievements instead were centrally attributed to the activists' ability to build bridges and coordinate a broad movement (I9a/IT/EP). Similarly, another eco-pacifist activist in 2015 highlights the role of external developments in the GJM's significant growth; in particular the Millennium Development Goals agreed upon in 2000 are described as very 'conducive' to the GJM as they triggered debates about development aid and trade justice (I10b/IT/EP-10). On the contrary, in 2011 the same activists largely attributed achievement of building a broad movement to a joint 'trial and error process' based on the shared understanding that it is time to come together and disclose the GJM's capacity 'to change things' (I10a/IT/EP-23). And also an anti-capitalist activist in 2015 de-emphasises the GJM's efforts in building a broad coalition by arguing that 'it's easy to stay together if all grow' (I16b/IT/AC-55), while in 2011 the same person emphasised how the counter-summit in Genoa unveiled the 'power' of the movement (I16a/IT/AC-12).

Furthermore, continuities with previous and later mobilisations tend to be more strongly emphasised in follow-up interviews in 2015 than in 2011. With respect to previous mobilisations, for example, an anti-capitalist activist in 2015 stresses that in Italy 'in general the left has been strong since the Second World War' (I17b/IT/AC-42) and describes how various left groups built a 'fertile ground for Seattle' (I17b/IT/AC-40). While in 2011 the same person rather stressed the weakness of the left in Italy linked to the 'defeat of the 70s' and recalled how surprisingly new the idea of a global day of action in Seattle was to the *Centri Sociali* (I17a/IT/AC; see full quote in chapter 3, p. 72).

With respect to boundaries between the GJM and later mobilisations, continuities of the GJM are more prominent in 2015 than in 2011, while activists in 2015 do share the view that the GJM is over (see chapter 2). In this vein, an eco-pacifist activist in 2015 emphasises with respect to current mobilisations that 'in terms of contents, its 100 percent a story of continuity' (I9b/IT/EP-8), whereas in 2011 the same person stressed that since the 2003 demonstrations 'it's a completely different situation' because of the more local and grassroots level of mobilisation, but also because of changes in issues addressed such as migration and environment (I9a/IT/EP-46). Similarly, an anti-capitalist activist in 2015 – while continuing to stress tactical differences – highlights the thematic continuities between the GJM and current struggles more than in 2011. This activist underlines in 2015 that the struggles against the European economic and democratic 'crisis' confirm that the GJM was 'right and that what we were starting to see was those mechanisms being applied at home' (I17b/IT/AC-30), while in 2011 the same person argued that present mobilisations in Europe are 'about new social struggles' (I17a/IT/AC-19).

CONCLUSION

This chapter showed how closely intertwined sharing a particular story is with movement identity. I demonstrated that the 'GJM narrative' is specific to a particular group of activists and to a particular period of time. The GJM narrative was developed and maintained by GJM activists over several years as part of the movement's collective meaning making until the point when a new cycle of mobilisation or other engagements became more salient. Furthermore, I showed that the GJM narrative is specific to activists who feel like part of the GJM at large. Activists primarily considering themselves part of specific GJM groups and those who no longer feel like part of the GJM tend to tell different stories about the GJM. Specifically, the GJM narrative's clear boundaries drawn between previous and later mobilisations as well as its distinct turning points are missing in the latter cases. These findings reveal that the more distant an activist felt to the GJM, the more the GJM narrative lost its edge, blurring the outlines of the GJM in terms of its time frame, its major characteristics and its agency. This underlines the central role that shared narratives play in defining commonalities and in forming and maintaining movement identity.

The chapter first demonstrated that GJM activists had shared central elements of the GJM narrative since the early years of the GJM. Drawing on a comparison of the interviews conducted in 2011 and 2012 with GJM publications from the late 1990s to the early 2000s, I illustrated the considerable continuity in how activists describe the GJM's developments and achievements. In particular, the distinct boundaries drawn between the GJM and previous mobilisations as well as the turning points identified with respect to overcoming left divides and neoliberal hegemony had already existed from early on. This showed how a certain plot was maintained over several years.

Second, I demonstrated how activists who primarily consider themselves part of specific GJM groups or who no longer feel part of the GJM do not share central elements of the GJM narrative. These activists' narratives miss the latter's clear boundary drawn between the GJM and other movements as well as its GJM-specific turning points. Developments and events within the GJM's cycle of mobilisation can hence be interpreted in very different ways beyond country- and sector-specific perspectives elaborated in chapter 2 – as successes or failures, as continuations or as breaks. Activists who primarily consider themselves part of a specific GJM group tell narratives about this group rather than about the GJM at large, and they accordingly tend to emphasise group-specific turning points and continuities with prior and later mobilisations. Activists who no longer feel like part of the GJM in 2011/2012 as well as in 2015 instead fail to identify boundaries and turning points altogether owing to doubts about the GJM's success in challenging neoliberal hegemony and overcoming divisions in the left.

More generally, these findings point to the central role that shared narratives play in forming and maintaining movement identity. It showed how the GJM narrative defined commonalities across diverse contexts and was shared by GJM activists as long as they felt like part of the GJM at large. This showed not only how activists can feel part of the larger movement to different degrees, but also that sharing the GJM narrative is connected with sharing GJM identity. Feeling like part of the GJM is of course not the same as collective identity since the former refers to an individual level of meaning making and the latter to a collective level (see chapter 1). However, the former provides a good insight into how far activists share a broader GJM discourse and the collective definitions of commonalities it entails; that is, it is an indicator of whether activists share the broader GJM identity. The finding that only activists who felt like part of the GJM at large shared the GJM narrative hence indicates that this shared narrative plays a central role in forming and maintaining movement identity.

This chapter also highlighted the durability of narratives over time. In addition to the malleability of narratives stressed in chapter 3, narratives can also have a certain element of stability. I showed accordingly how a certain plot was maintained over several years, while the individual events associated with the plot's episodes partly changed. Hence, the patterns of emplotting and interpreting the GJM's events remained remarkably similar over time.

Linked to this narrative continuity, the chapter also revealed the continuing significance of the GJM narrative across various stages in the movement's cycle of mobilisation. Hence, stories of success are not only told after a phase of mobilisation reached its definite peak, but already early on. In this vein, I showed how early and relatively small events are considered to be turning points in the case of the European GJM. Group memory thus does not require many years of joint mobilisation, nor is it added only in retrospect. Instead, it can also be created at the very beginning of a mobilisation cycle on the basis of a first event that is thought to be influential. The continuing relevance of the GJM narrative furthermore shows how narratives that distinguish one's own movement from previous mobilisations are not only relevant in the beginning of a cycle of mobilisation; they are also subsequently relevant.

At the same time, this chapter also illuminated how the meaning and significance of certain events can change over time. A comparison of the findings in this chapter with those in chapter 3 reveal in particular how some events become more important over the years while others become less prominent or disappear from activists' narratives. For example, the demonstrations against the war in Iraq in 2003 have tended to disappear over the years in narratives by German activists. While still prominently mentioned in early publications, in the interviews in 2011 and 2012, these protests are much less prominent, especially among anti-capitalist activists (see chapter 3). Similarly, Polish activists tend to attribute more significance in early publications to international GJM events and in particular to the first ESF in Florence in 2002 than in the interviews in 2011 and 2012 (see chapter 3). More research on the continuities and changes in activists' narratives over time would be valuable.

NOTES

1. Activists developed their interpretations of GJM events in a variety of debates, publications, films and events in interaction with those in media and public discourse. While limited to interviews with activists, the present analysis of central GJM publications allows accessing this broader discourse to some extent. On the controversial

interpretation of, for example, the counter-summit in Genoa, see Niwot (2011), Vicari (2015) and Daphi (2017).

2. All translations in this first part of the chapter by the author.

3. In addition, publications after the counter-summit in Genoa, of course, also stress that many things still need to be done, claiming that 'we have a densely packed agenda' (Doc10-IT, p. 8), in particular the need to continue the broad coalition (Doc12-IT, p. 5) and 'hold together different intentions' (Doc10-IT, p. 6).

4. Social anti-globalism here most probably meant to refer to non-institutionalised groups opposing neoliberal globalisation.

5. This distinction bases on the statements made during the interviews about belongingness (see details below) and may of course vary over time.

6. This concerns a small group among the sixty-seven activists interviewed in 2011 and 2012 across the three countries and sectors (see details in appendix A). These interviewees consider themselves primarily as members of a certain group within the GJM. They may also consider themselves part of the GJM more generally; however, their own group is considerably more central to them. Accordingly, these activists refer only to their own group and its activities by using 'us' or 'we', whereas the GJM and its activities rather are referred to as 'them'.

7. This concerns a small group among the sixty-seven activists interviewed in 2011 and 2012 across the three countries and sectors, who in contrast to the majority of interviewees stated that they once did consider themselves part of the GJM, but no longer do (see details in appendix A). Some of them are no longer politically active at all; others changed to more institutionalised groups or other issues.

8. In order to maintain the anonymity of the interviewee, the original source from 2001 cannot be disclosed here.

9. The follow-up interviews concern a small group of activists in Italy who shared the GJM narrative in interviews conducted in 2011 and who was interviewed again in 2015 using the same questionnaire (see details in appendix A). Since the aim of the follow-up interviews was to explore changes in activists' narratives about the GJM in the context of a new cycle of mobilisation, interviews focused on activists in Italy due to their overall stronger involvement in and proximity to European anti-austerity protests than their German and Polish counterparts (see e.g., Flesher Fominaya, 2017; della Porta & Andretta, 2013). Interviewees continued to be active in 2015 in various movement groups, addressing also issues of austerity. Furthermore, the follow-up interviews focused on activists from the anti-capitalist and eco-pacifist sectors, the two sectors set most apart in Italy in order to be able to identify sectorial differences in changes of narratives over time.

Conclusion

Narrative Identity and Movement Continuity

Most social movements bring together a diverse crowd and require activists to work across considerable differences in sociocultural backgrounds, political traditions and organisational routines. In order to understand how activist cooperation works despite such diversity, it is important to explore how commonalities are created across differences. Activists' collective actions and continued commitment depend on the commonalities they recognise among each other. The book's findings highlighted the role that especially narratives play in defining such commonalities, in integrating divergent interests and approaches into a collective identity. I showed in particular how a shared narrative helped to bridge the considerable national and sectorial differences within the European GJM and to form and maintain a transnational movement identity. The power of this shared 'GJM narrative' draws on its broad, overarching plot which allowed creating a sense of shared experience and agency without negating differences.

These findings not only contribute to a better understanding of the link between collective identity and narrative and of how movement identity is formed and maintained, but also help comprehend other dimensions of contentious politics such as movements' strategies and durability. In the following, I will first summarise the main findings of the book and then discuss implications of these findings with respect to collective identity, movement durability, tactical decisions as well as transformative effects of protest events.

SUMMARY: THE ROLE OF STORIES IN DEFINING COMMONALITIES

Drawing on a socio-constructionist definition and a narrative approach to collective identity, this book set out to explore the stories activists tell about their movement and the role these stories play in building movement identity. Based on over seventy interviews and focus groups I conducted with GJM activists in Germany, Italy and Poland in 2011, 2012 and 2015, as well as an analysis of GJM publications, the book revealed both differences and remarkable similarities in the narratives activists tell about the GJM. The book's analysis showed that while there are considerable differences in narratives as activists focus on different events and actors, activists also share a 'GJM narrative' across sectors and countries in terms of a broad joint plot.

In the first empirical chapter (chapter 2) , I demonstrated the differences in activists' narratives about the GJM with respect to actors and events considered central. Such differences partly correspond with the various national and sectorial constellations, but they are also are a matter of active, group-specific meaning making and selection of relevant past events. On the one hand, I identified national differences as activists in Italy, Germany and Poland focus primarily on GJM developments in their respective countries and have divergent accounts of the movement's successes, major events and major groups. Furthermore, narratives differ between the three countries with respect to their degree of congruence, as activists agree on central actors and events more in some cases (especially in Italy) and less in others (especially in Poland). These national differences underline the significance of national and local contexts of mobilisation in transnational social movements.

On the other hand, I identified sectorial patterns in narratives that are similar across all three countries. Activists refer most prominently and most explicitly to events and groups closest to themselves in terms of organisation, ideas and tactics. Differences were found in particular between the anti-neoliberal, eco-pacifist and anti-capitalist sectors of the GJM. For example, social forums are much more prominent in narratives by more moderate activists from the first two sectors, while activists from the anti-capitalist sector put much more emphasis on counter-summits.

The second empirical chapter (chapter 3) in contrast revealed the commonalities rather than differences in activists' narratives about the GJM across countries and sectors. I showed that while there are country- and sector-specific differences in activists' narratives with regard to events and actors considered central, the overall narrative is very similar. Activists in this vein were demonstrated to share a specific 'GJM narrative' that integrates the country- and sector-specific experiences and perspectives into a shared plot with a sequence of four episodes. The four episodes comprise: (1) a situation prior to the GJM's beginning which is characterised by a weak and divided left and the hegemony of neoliberalism; (2) a build-up episode describing a process of learning in which the GJM starts to grow, in particular with respect to transnational cooperation, but remains limited in its success to overcome divisions in the left and to challenge neoliberal hegemony; (3) a peak episode in which the GJM reaches its full potential and succeeds in overcoming neoliberal hegemony and left divides and (4) the GJM's decline and end as marked by its decreasing capacity for cross-sectorial and transnational mobilisation. I showed how this plot creates a notion of shared experience, namely regarding the joint experience of initial failures and later successes in challenging neoliberal hegemony and overcoming divisions within the left. Such a notion, I pointed out, helps to delineate the GJM's central characteristics vis-à-vis others and to highlight its agency.

In the third empirical chapter (chapter 4) I showed how closely the 'GJM narrative' is connected with building and maintaining collective identity in the GJM. I demonstrated that the narrative identified in chapter 3 is specific to a particular group in a particular period of time, namely the GJM's cycle of mobilisation and the years immediately following. Drawing on a comparison of interviews I conducted in 2011 and 2012 with central GJM publications between 1997 and 2005, I first revealed that the GJM narrative identified in chapter 3 is similar not only across sectors and countries but also across time. It had been developed and maintained by GJM activists since the GJM's early years. Second, I showed that only activists who consider themselves part of the GJM at large share the GJM narrative. Activists who primarily consider themselves part of a specific GJM group or who no longer feel part of the GJM tell different kinds of stories about the GJM. Notably, the GJM narrative's clear boundaries drawn between previous mobilisations as well as its distinct turning points are missing in these narratives. This chapter hence demonstrated that, despite a considerable durability of the GJM narrative over time, activists shared this narrative only as long as they felt like part of the GJM at large, pointing to the major role this narrative played in forming and maintaining GJM identity.

MOVEMENT IDENTITY, NARRATIVE AND MEMORY

The book's findings highlight the central role of narratives in forming and maintaining collective identity in social movements. In this way, I not only stressed narratives' general ability to create a sense of shared experience, a collective past, that allows an integration of the diverse, specific experiences of mobilisation, whether they are shaped by a country's political condition, a sector's ideological vision, a group's tactical preferences or an individual's motivation. I also demonstrated the close link between sharing a specific narrative and movement identity by comparing narratives across different degrees of activists' belongingness. Activists' relationships to a movement can vary as activists can be more singularly committed or less (see e.g.,

Downton & Wehr, 1997; King, 2004) and hence the extent to which activists share a movement identity will vary. By showing that only activists who felt like part of the GJM at large shared the collective 'GJM narrative', I underlined the vital role this narrative played in forming and maintaining GJM identity. While activists involved in and feeling part of the GJM shared the GJM narrative for many years, they ceased to do so once they no longer felt part of the GJM and turned their attention to other engagements. Central elements of this shared narrative were already found early in the GJM's cycle of mobilisation suggesting that they preceded the formation of GJM identity; however, further research would be required to ascertain such a causal link.

The book's findings contribute to our understanding of how forming and maintaining collective identity in social movements work. First of all, they highlight the role of implicit and latent elements in building identity in addition to explicit arguments about problems and solutions stressed in most existing research about movement identity (see chapter 1). Exploring commonalities constructed in narratives of shared experience reveal insights into 'persuasion and shared vision at more subtle, imaginative and pre-prepositional levels' (Davis, 2002, p. 24). Furthermore, as I will elaborate below, the book's findings underline the interplay of cognitive, relational and emotional dimensions in collective identity formation and indicate that particular kinds of narratives are particularly conducive to building and maintaining movement identity, namely group memories with a plot that delineates a specific sequence of episodes.

Movement Identity Beyond Shared Goals

As discussed in chapter 1, existing research on movement identity tends to focus on either the cognitive, relational or emotional dimensions of collective identity. Existing research especially concentrates on the role of activists' shared framing of problems and goals in forming identity. This is in contrast to the argument of several movement scholars that activists need to do more than agree on goals to form collective identity and engage in collective action (e.g., Rucht, 1995; Davis, 2002; Polletta, 1998a, 2006). By revealing the central role of narratives in building movement identity, this book instead demonstrated how cognitive, relational and emotional dimensions are intertwined in forming and maintaining collective identity. Hence, in addition to shared cognitions about problems and goals, movement identity was shown to draw on social boundaries and emotional proximity, which provides a fruitful addition to the existing research.

In this vein, this book demonstrated how narratives of shared experience delineate commonalities within the GJM with respect to shared cognitions, boundaries and emotional proximity (see chapter 3). Especially the notion of sharing the experience of successfully challenging neoliberal hegemony and overcoming divisions within the left played a vital role in defining these commonalities. Accordingly, I first showed how the narrative underlines the GJM's shared master frame of anti-neoliberalism. In the first three episodes the opposition to neoliberalism is outlined as the central challenge that the GJM faces. In addition to the overall significance of shared cognitions about problems and goals, this finding highlights how such cognitions do not necessarily need to be formulated explicitly but can also be expressed more implicitly through narrative plots.

Second, I demonstrated how the GJM narrative's emphasis on joint experiences in challenging neoliberal hegemony and overcoming left divisions drew clear boundaries between the GJM and other actors. On the one hand, the narratives underlined the distance from the agents of neoliberal globalisation. On the other hand, they distinguished the GJM from previous and later movements, which activists consider less successful in challenging neoliberal policies (in particular movements prior to the GJM) and in building a broad left coalition (movements both before and after the GJM). These distinctions between the GJM and previous and especially later movements refer more to differences in political impact, transnational exchange and coalition building rather than to goals. In fact, the frame of anti-neoliberalism is seen to continue especially in later mobilisations with respect to the critique of deficits in social justice and democratic participation (see chapters 2 and 3).

Third, I showed how the shared sense of experience in the 'GJM narrative' fostered and expressed emotional proximity between GJM activists through its emphasis on both shared hardship and triumph. This first concerned a shared range of emotions such as feelings of disappointment and frustrations that activists emphasise in the context of the joint distress experienced as the omnipresence of neoliberal thought and left divisions posed obstacles to mobilisation. Second, it concerned shared feelings of joy and pride that activists stress with respect to the GJM's ability to mobilise broadly and to yield positive public resonance despite these obstacles.

The book's analysis of activists' narratives, hence, provided considerable insights into the interplay of cognitive, relational and emotional elements in forming collective identity. The data analysed, however, do have certain limits. First, the interviews, focus groups and publications allowed accessing the re-enactment and reproduction of cognitions, boundaries and emotional proximity in narratives rather than accessing their embodied experiences directly as enactment approaches to movement identity do (see chapter 1). Second, the data allowed only limited insights into how activists' narratives were developed in interaction with outsider's definitions of the GJM, for example, in the media. While beyond the scope of the book, more research on this interaction would be valuable.

Identity Narratives

In addition to highlighting the interplay of cognitive, relational and emotional dimensions in forming collective identity, the book's analysis also indicates that certain kinds of narratives are especially vital to building and maintaining movement identity, namely group memories with a specific plot. This finding contributes to the literature on movement identity as well as to the broader literature on identity and narrative. As elaborated in chapter 1, particularly the latter literature is ambiguous about which qualities a narrative requires to foster collective identity. Scholars disagree about whether a coherent narrative with a clear agency or a more open narrative with a general shared theme is more conducive to forming and maintaining collective identity (see chapter 1). This book suggests that narratives which combine a broad notion of shared experience and agency with the plurality of individual- and group-specific perspectives are particularly central to movement identity. I demonstrated how GJM activists shared a broad, overarching plot to which the different specific GJM experiences and events could be linked. Accordingly, events in each episode of the plot were shown to differ, but the characteristics ascribed to each episode were strikingly similar across countries, sectors and time. In this way, the GJM narrative integrated the country- and sector-specific GJM experiences without negating differences.

The book's findings furthermore point to the importance of narrative structures as they emphasise the vital role of a narrative plot with a specific sequence of episodes. This goes beyond a shared plot in terms of a general theme. I showed in this vein how the shared GJM plot comprised four distinct episodes that not only drew clear boundaries between the GJM, on the one hand, and previous and later movements, on the other, but also identified a distinct turning point and a conversion of the prior situation with respect to the movement at large. As I elaborated, this narrative plot played a crucial role in forming and maintaining collective identity as it created a sense of shared experience and agency, constituting a collective story of becoming. While some elements of this 'GJM narrative' will most probably be unique to this movement – especially the emphasis on overcoming neoliberal hegemony and left divisions – collective narratives with a plot that similarly draws clear boundaries and identifies distinct turning points can also be expected to play a central role in building collective identity in other social movements.

With regard to the narrative boundaries drawn, I demonstrated how activists across countries and sectors contrast the GJM with a prior situation, exhibiting the tendency to exaggerate previous left weaknesses and to neglect existing left critique of neoliberal globalisation prior to the GJM. This distancing highlighted, as I showed, the GJM's ability to build broad left coalitions and challenge the hegemony of neoliberalism. This served to stress the GJM's novelty and noteworthiness as also shown in the case of other movements (see chapter 3).

In addition to such boundaries, the book demonstrated the powerful role a plot with a turning point relating to the GJM at large can play in building collective identity. I accordingly revealed that only GJM activists who felt like part of the GJM overall identified such a turning point in their narratives (see chapter 4). Only these activists' narratives contained a turning point that describes a moment of collective rather than individual and movement- rather than group-specific conversion:[1] it describes the change of the GJM from an inexistent and then marginal player to an agent capable of changing neoliberal realities. Such a turning point is critical to collective identity formation not only because it marks differences between the GJM and prior movements, but also because it defines collective achievements creating a sense of collective agency and success.

More generally, the book's findings about the role of group memories highlight the importance of memories in social movements, in particular memories about the movement itself. Research on narratives and identity here can profit from the literature on collective memory as it draws attention to the role of a narrative's content and collectivity in building collective identity. Studies on memory in movements in turn can profit from the former literature's attention to narrative structure. In addition to analysing the structure of GJM narratives, this book underlined the significance of *collective* narratives in building movement identity, calling attention to the importance of processes of collective – as opposed to individual – meaning making and to the collective practices and rituals involved in these processes. Specifically unreflected rituals and practices deserve more scholarly interest (see also e.g., Flesher Fominaya, 2014, 2016). Furthermore, the book's findings stress that a certain content of narratives is vital to forming collective identity, namely that it makes a difference whether one tells one's story about the movement's emergence or about some other actor's development. Narratives creating a sense of collective history are very powerful in forming collective identity.

NARRATIVES AND MOVEMENT CONTINUITY

Beyond the insights into the formation of collective identity, the book also has implications for questions relating to movement continuity. As I will elaborate below, the book's findings in particular contribute to three aspects of movement continuity: first, to the durability of movements overall; second, to continuities and changes of movements within a cycle of mobilisation; and third, to continuities and changes between different cycles of mobilisation.

Identity Narratives and Movement Durability

Social movement scholars have been interested for many years in what makes social movements durable, why some movements survive only briefly, while others last many years. Sharing a collective identity has been found to be vital for making movements more durable as it fosters activists' commitment (e.g., Whittier, 1997; Passy & Giugni, 2000). The book's findings contribute to this literature by offering insights into how the collective identity underlying such continued commitment endures over time, a question often neglected in studies about movement durability (see also Gongaware, 2011). I showed in particular how GJM identity was maintained over many years based on a broad narrative plot capable of adapting to new developments and events. The analysis in this vein revealed the continuing significance of the 'GJM narrative' throughout the movement's cycle of mobilisation and the years immediately after to activists considering themselves part of the GJM. The book hence highlighted the central role identity narratives play in making movements more enduring.

The continuity of the 'GJM narrative' throughout the GJM mobilisation cycle furthermore demonstrates the stability of certain collective narratives over time. This reveals how canonical the GJM narrative became within the movement and how it may have thereby also constrained other interpretations of past activities. As all stories are developed and shared in reference to stories heard before, a prominent general narrative can complicate recounting the past differently and can in this way be a constraint as well as an enabler of individual activists' activities.[2] My analysis has shown how indeed some events and actors are overlooked in the GJM narrative as it 'crowded out more complex stories' (Armstrong & Crage, 2006, p. 743). This concerned, for example, the neglect of autonomist groups linked to PGA in the German GJM (see chapter 2). Overall, however, the book focused on the role of activists' narratives in empowering rather than constraining activists and in enabling the formation of collective identity. Accordingly, it also concentrated more on agreement than conflict about how to interpret the past, owing to the book's interest in how activists identify commonalities. The trade-off between enabling and constraining qualities of shared narratives and the conflicts this entails are worth more investigation in future studies.

Continuities and Changes within Cycles of Mobilisation

The findings of this book have implications for understanding movement continuity also in another sense, namely, with respect to the continuities and changes of movements within a cycle of mobilisation. The book in particular draws attention to the role of identity narratives in choices of protest tactics and in the transformative effects of protest events in the course of such a cycle.

Identity and Strategy: The Path Dependency of Repertoires

Strategy and identity have long been considered in opposition to each other as scholars distinguished between expressive dimensions of movements, on the one hand, and strategic action, on the other (e.g., Cohen, 1985; Jenkins, 1983). More recently, however, scholars have increasingly emphasised how closely movement identity and strategies are linked. They have not only shown that identities can be employed strategically (e.g., Bernstein, 1997); strategic choices have also been demonstrated to centrally draw on collective identity. This has been revealed in particular with respect to protest repertoires, that is, the established constellation of tactics developed and maintained by movements (Tilly, 1995, p. 43; Tarrow, 1998). Various scholars have accordingly stressed that social movements adopt certain protest tactics not only because they are thought to be internally or externally effective, but also because they resonate with a movement's overall culture and identity (e.g., Wood, 2007; Taylor & van Dyke, 2008; Stekelenburg, 2014; McGarry & Jasper, 2015). The book's findings contribute to these insights on repertoire choices by illuminating how activists identify such resonance in narratives and how they combine it with considerations about internal and external effectiveness.

I have shown in this vein how narratives about movements' past activities shape which actions are considered suitable and effective and which are not. This preselects possible future repertoires and thus affects tactical decisions. Stories in this way 'limit what happens next' (Tilly, 2002, p. 9). A sense of success will increase the likelihood of similar tactics being used again, while notions of defeat will instead decrease such odds. This underlines the path dependency of repertoires: protest tactics are not simply a toolbox from which activists independently choose, but their selection is crucially shaped by previous tactical choices and their retrospective interpretations.

While this book's analysis did not focus in particular on how tactics are remembered, it highlighted the insights an analysis of narratives about a movement's past activities can provide into repertoire decisions. For example, the book's analysis of activists' narratives points to how activists' evaluated the counter-summit in Seattle in 1999 as a suitable expression of the movements' 'new politics' and as very effective (see chapter 3) and how this may be connected to the centrality of the tactic of counter-summits in the following years. More research is required on the connections between the narratives activists tell about their activities and repertoire choices.

The Mediated Effects of Protest Events

The book's demonstration of the importance of protests' retrospect interpretations also has implications for understanding the transformative effects of protest events. The growing literature on transformative effects emphasises that protests not only increase the external visibility of social movements' claims and demands, but also have an internal impact on them, shaping movements' organisation, goals, repertoires and identity. Several movement scholars have accordingly shown how protest events produce a need for coordination and create intensive exchanges between activists that change cultural and social meaning, bring forth debates on new issues, trigger new protest tactics, create and sustain networks, facilitate mutual learning as well as strengthen collective identity (e.g., della Porta, 2008, 2011; Vicari, 2015; Sewell, 1996; McAdam & Sewell, 2001).

In addition to underlining the impact protest events have on building and maintaining collective identity (see also della Porta, 2008, 2011; Daphi, 2017), the book's findings contribute to this literature in particular by emphasising the interpretational dimension of transformative effects, that is, the role that actors' interpretations play in the impact of events on movements. How are the experiences during an event transferred to later interactions and future mobilisations? In former studies, the transformative effect of protest events is often attributed to the immediate effects of intensive face-to-face exchange. The book's findings instead stress the role of more mediated effects in terms of the activists' retrospective interpretations of events in narratives. These findings highlighted the central role that the retrospective interpretations of events play in forming a sense of shared experience and delineating shared cognitions, social boundaries and emotional proximity. The findings also showed variety of events can assume a major role – a 'cardinal function' – within such narratives, not only the largest (e.g., the anti-war demonstrations in 2003), but, for example, also the most controversial (e.g., the counter-summit in Genoa in 2001), or the closest (e.g., the counter-summit in Warsaw in 2004).

The consideration of such narratively mediated effects also helps, to some extent, avoiding the overemphasis on visible and extraordinary elements in social movements at the expense of more latent and everyday processes, a tendency for which the literature on social movements and especially the literature on transformative effects has been criticised.[3] Narratives connect the extraordinariness of protest events to the ordinariness of social movements' everyday life. Through narratives protest events are reconstructed and relived later on, even during phases of abeyance (Taylor, 1989) in which movements are less active or reorient themselves.

Continuities and Changes between Different Cycles of Mobilisation

Last but not least, I would like to draw attention to the insights that the analysis of activists' narratives offers into continuities and changes *between* different cycles of mobilisation. Social movements hardly start from scratch, and hence each new generation of activists has to define its relationship with previous mobilisations (see also Zamponi & Daphi, 2014). The analysis of activists' narratives about past mobilisations helps understand which forms of organisation, which topics and which tactics are picked up in subsequent mobilisation cycles and which are discarded. Activists' memories of past movements provide insights into which elements activists consider worthy of continuation and the reasons why. Further research on such narratives would hence be valuable for improving our understanding of continuities and discontinuities between different cycles of mobilisation.

The book pointed to the continuities which activists who were both involved in the GJM and in the later anti-austerity protests in Europe identify between both cycles of mobilisation. As I demonstrated, activists stress in particular the continuing concern with issues of social justice and deficits in democratic participation (see chapter 3). However, the later cycle of mobilisation is described to seek more local and concrete solutions to these issues, which activists consider more effective than the GJM's broader and transnational approach. In the context of the current political shift to the right in Europe and beyond, it remains to be seen which forms of past activist organisation, topics and tactics will be discarded or revived in reaction and opposition to such developments.

NOTES

1. See, for example, Rappaport (1993) on individual conversion stories in the context of self-help groups and Guzik and Golier (2004) on individual conversion stories in the context of feminist movements.

2. On narratives as constraints, see, for example, Polletta et al. (2011), Benford (2002), Davis (2002), Tilly (2002) and Jasper and McGarry (2015).

3. See, for example, Haug (2013) and Flesher Fominaya (2014, 2015).

Acknowledgements

This book developed in many different places, with interview locations ranging from abandoned bunkers to bustling campaign offices and cozy living rooms, and with countless hours spent in libraries and offices in Berlin, Florence, Frankfurt, London and Warsaw. But above all, this effort was made possible by the support of numerous people. My first thanks go to the many activists who took the time to share their experiences and insights with me and without whom this book would not have been written. I am also sincerely grateful to my doctoral supervisors Klaus Eder, Dieter Rucht and Donatella della Porta for their sustained support and indispensable feedback. In addition, I would like to offer great thanks to the numerous colleagues at the Centre on Social Movement Studies in Florence, the Institute for Protest and Social Movement Studies in Berlin and elsewhere, who supported this book through inspiring discussions and constructive comments. I am particularly indebted to James Jasper, Lorenzo Zamponi, Grzegorz Piotrowski, Nicole Doerr, Simon Teune, Cristina Flesher Fominaya, Sebastian Haunss and Britta Baumgarten. My gratitude also goes to Nicole Deitelhoff and her team at the University of Frankfurt, where I completed the final manuscript of this book.

I thank the *German National Academic Foundation* for providing the financial resources for this research through a doctoral scholarship. The *Alexander von Humboldt Foundation* offered a generous *Feodor-Lynen Research Fellowship* in 2015, for which I extend my gratitude. I also thank Jeffrey Purchla for his careful proofreading of the manuscript and the team from Rowman & Littlefield International for their support along the way. I furthermore owe thanks to Anna Dolinska and Lorena de Vita for their practical assistance during fieldwork in Poland and Italy. And I offer my full appreciation to the staff of the Berlin Graduate School of Social Sciences at the Humboldt-University Berlin for their friendly logistical support.

Last but not least, I express my deepest gratitude to my family and friends for their moral and practical support during the process of writing this book as well as for the many pleasant distractions. I thank in particular my parents, Dorothee and Jochen, as well as Alex and Nele.

Appendix A

Interviews and Focus Groups With GJM Activists

Table AppA.1   List of Interviews and Focus Groups by Country, Interview Date, and Sector

ITALY (IT)		Date	*Primary affiliation 2000–2003* [a]
Interviews (I)			
AN	1 [b]	May 2011	COBAS
	2 [b]	May 2011	FIOM
	3 [b]	May 2011	Genoa Social Forum
	4 [b]	June 2011	Rifondazione Comunista
	5 [b]	June 2011	Attac
	6 [d]	June 2011	Rifondazione Comunista
EP	7 [b]	April 2011	Beati construttori di pace
	8 [b]	April 2011	ARCI
	9 [b+e]	May 2011	ARCI
	10 [b+e]	June 2011	Debt relief campaign
	11 [b]	June 2011	Pax Christi
	12 [c]	June 2011	Emergency
	13 [c]	June 2011	Marcia delle donne
	14 [c]	June 2011	Legambiente
AC	15	April 2011	Tute Bianche/Disobbedienti
	16 [b+e]	April 2011	Centro Sociale Southern Italy
	17 [b+e]	May 2011	Centro Sociale Rome
	18 [b]	May 2011	Centro Sociale Southern Italy
	19 [b]	May 2011	Student union
	20 [b]	June 2011	Tute Bianche/Disobbedienti

Focus Group Italy (FG/IT)			
AN	1	July 2011	FIOM
EP	2		Rete Lilliput
ACa	3		Giovani Comunisti
ACb	4		Centro Sociale Southern Italy

GERMANY (DE)		Date	*Primary affiliation 2000–2003* [a]
Interviews (I)			
AN	1 [b]	Sept. 2011	Attac
	2 [b]	Feb. 2012	WEED
	3 [c]	Feb. 2012	Attac
	4 [d]	Feb. 2012	Attac
	5 [b]	March 2012	Attac
	6 [b]	March 2012	Ver.di
	7 [c]	April 2012	IG-Metall
	8 [b]	April 2012	Die Linke
EP	9 [b]	Feb. 2011	Kairos Europa
	10 [b]	Feb. 2011	Environmental group
	11 [b]	Feb. 2012	Netzwerk Friedenskooperative
	12 [b]	Feb. 2012	Informationsstelle Lateinamerika
	13 [b]	April 2012	Pax Christi
	14 [d]	April 2012	Kairos Europa
	15 [c]	April 2012	BUND
	16 [c]	April 2012	Evangelische Entwicklungsdienst e.V.

AC	17 [c]	Jan. 2011	BUKO
	18 [c]	Feb. 2011	Ya Basta Network Germany
	19	Feb. 2011	IL
	20 [b]	Aug. 2011	PGA
	21 [b]	Feb. 2012	SAV
	22	March 2012	PGA
	23 [b]	April 2012	IL
	24 [b]	April 2012	Antifaschistische Linke Berlin
	25 [b]	April 2012	No Lager
	26	April 2012	Linksruck/Marx21

Focus Group Germany (FG/DE)

AN	1	May 2011	Attac
EP	2		Environmental group
AC	3		Linksruck/Marx21

POLAND (PL)		Date	Primary affiliation 2000–2003[a]
Interviews (I)			
AN	1	Oct. 2011	Attac
	2 [b]	Nov. 2011	Nowa Lewica
	3 [b]	Nov. 2011	Publishing project
	4 [b]	Nov. 2011	Młodzi Socialiści
	5 [d]	Nov. 2011	Młodzi Socialiści
	6 [b]	Nov. 2011	Artist collective
	7	Nov. 2011	Sierpien80
	8 [d]	Nov. 2011	Student union
	9 [c]	Nov. 2011	Krytyka Polityczna
	10 [c]	Nov. 2011	Młodzi Socialiści
	11 [c]	Nov. 2011	Attac
	12 [b]	Nov. 2011	Attac
EP	13 [c]	Nov. 2011	Zieloni2004
	14 [d]	Dec. 2011	Lepszy Świat
AC	15 [b]	Oct. 2011	Anarcho-syndicalist group
	16 [b]	Oct. 2011	Lewicowa Alternatywa
	17 [b]	Nov. 2011	Federacja Anarchistyczna
	18	Dec. 2011	Anarchist group
	19 [b]	Dec. 2011	Pracownicza Demokracja
	20 [b]	Dec. 2011	Inicjatywa Pracownicza
	21 [c]	Dec. 2011	Inicjatywa Pracownicza

Focus Group Poland (FG/PL)

AN	1	Dec. 2011	Krytyka Polityczna
EP	2		Amnesty International
AC	3		Federacja Anarchistyczna

[a] Main affiliation as stated by the activists (for Germany 2000–2005). To maintain anonymity, only one affiliation is listed here, though many activists have two or more. For the same reason, only general group descriptions are provided in some cases, rather than specific group names.

[b] Interviews included in the quantitative analysis in chapter 2.

[c] Activists who during the interview expressed feeling primarily like part of certain groups within the GJM, rather than of the GJM at large (see analysis in chapter 4).

[d] Activists who during the interview expressed feeling no longer like part of the GJM (see analysis in chapter 4).

[e] Follow-up interviews conducted in June 2015.

Appendix B

Selection of GJM Documents

Table AppB.1 List of Selected GJM Publications by Country[a]

ITALY (IT)

Title	Description	Authors/Editors	Date/source
Peoples' Global Action Archive/Italy	Online collection of reports and reflections about GJM protests by Italian activists	Contributions by Italian grassroots activists	2000–2002 https://www.nadir.org/nadir/initiativ/agp/en/
Granello di Sabbia	Bi-weekly newsletter of *Attac Italy*	Edited by *Attac Italy* Contributions by GJM activists from different sectors	Issues 1–78 (Sept. 2001–Dec. 2002)
Zona Rossa: le "quattro giornate di Napoli" contro il Global forum	Book	Edited and contributions by *La Rete No Global – Network Campano per i diritti globali*	2001 Publisher: DeriveApprodi
Genova - Il Libro Bianco	Magazine, supplement to the papers L'Unita, Liberazione, Il Manifesto, Carta	Edited by the communications group of *Ilan Social Forum* Contributions by GJM activists from different sectors	2002

GERMANY (DE)

Title	Description	Authors/Editors	Date/source
Analyse & Kritik. Zeitung für linke Debatte und Praxis	Monthly left paper	Contributions by GJM activists from different sectors	Issues 417–479 (Aug.1998–Dec. 2003)
Zeitschrift der deutschen Sektion der internationalen katholischen Friedensbewegung Pax Christi	Bi-monthly newsletter of the German chapter of Pax Christi	Edited and contributions by *Pax Christi Germany*	Issues 01_2000–05_2001 (Jan. 2000–Dec. 2001)
Sand im Getriebe. Internationaler deutschsprachiger Rundbrief der Attac-Bewegung	Monthly newsletter of *Attac Germany/Attac Austria/Attac Switzerland*	Edited by *Attac Germany/Attac Austria/Attac Switzerland*Contributions by GJM activists from different sectors	Issues 1–25 (Sept. 2001–July 2003)

Title	Description	Authors/Editors	Date/source
Nach Göteburg und Genua. Welche Taktik Braucht die Antikapitalistische Bewegung	Collection of essays	Edited and contributions by *Sozialistische Alternative*	2001
Die Ideen von Seattle und Genua. Eine Kritik der Kritiker	Book	Edited and contributions by *Sozialistische Alternative*	2002
Eine andere Welt ist möglich!	Book	Edited and contributions by *Attac Germany/Attac France*	2002 Publisher: VSA-Verlag
Unsere Welt ist keine Ware. Handbuch für Globalisierungskritiker	Book	Edited by *Linksruck* Contributions by GJM activists from different sectors	2002 Publisher: Kiepenheuer und Witsch Verlag
Radikal Global - Bausteine für eine internationalistische Linke	Book	Edited by BUKO Contributions by GJM activists from different sectors	2003 Publisher: Assoziation A Verlag

POLAND (PL)

Title	Description	Authors/Editors	Date/source
Attac Poland Archive	Online collection of essays & reports, including several reprints, in particular from the magazines *Robotnika Śląskiego* (Worker of Silesia) and later *Nowy Robotnik* (The New Worker) as well as from *lewica.pl*	Edited by *Attac Poland* (section "Publications & Documents") Contributions by GJM activists from different sectors	2000–2005 http://www.attac.pl/?lg=pl&kat=2&dzial=128 &typ=2

(Continued)

Table AppB.1   List of Selected GJM Publications by Country[a]   (Continued)

INTERNATIONAL (INT)

Title	Description	Author/Editor	Date/sources
Peoples' Global Action Bulletin	Intermittent newsletter	Edited by *Peoples' Global Action*; Contributions by grassroots activists worldwide	Issues 0–6 (Dec. 1997-Feb. 2000)https://www.nadir.org/nadir/initiativ/agp/en/#bul
Peoples' Global Action Archive	Online collection of reports and interviews about GJM protests worldwide	Contributions by grassroots activists worldwide	1998–2003https://www.nadir.org/nadir/initiativ/agp/en/
WSF documents I	Resolutions of the first, second, and third World Social Forums in Porto Alegre	Edited by World Social Forum	2001–2003
WSF documents II	Central speeches at the first, second, and third World Social Forums and related events	Contributions by international GJM activists from different sectors	2001–2003
We are everywhere: the irresistible rise of global anticapitalism	Book	Edited by collective *Notes from Nowhere*; Contributions by direct action activists worldwide	2003 Publisher: Verso
World Social Forum: Challenging Empires	Book	Edited by J. Sen, A. Anand, A. Escobar & P. Waterman; Contributions by international GJM activists from different sectors	2004 Publisher: Viveka Foundation

[a] Central publications were identified for each country based on expert interviews and the criterion of broad readership within the GJM as well as the consideration of different GJM sectors. In addition, especially those publications were selected that contained considerable elements of self-reflection in order to access activists' GJM stories.

Bibliography

Aguilar Fernández, P. & Humlebaek, C. (2002). Collective memory and national identity in the Spanish democracy: The legacies of francoism and the civil war. *History & Memory, 14*(1), 121–164.

Aminzade, R. & McAdam, D. (2001). Emotions and Contentious Politics. In R. Aminzade, D. McAdam, E. Perry, W. H. Sewell, S. Tarrow & C. Tilly (Eds.), *silence and Voice in the Study of Contentious Politics* (pp. 14–50). Cambridge, New York: Cambridge University Press.

Andretta, M., della Porta, D., Mosca, L., & Reiter, H. (2003). *No Global - New Global: Identität und Strategien der Antiglobalisierungsbewegung.* Frankfurt: Campus Verlag.

Anthias, F. (2002). Where do I belong? Narrating collective identity and translocational positionality. *Ethnicities, 2,* 491–514.

Antoniewicz, P. (2012). Anatomie der Antiglobalisierungsproteste in Polen. In D. Bingen, M. Jarosz & P. Loew (Eds.), *Legitimation und Protest Gesellschaftliche Unruhe in Polen, Ostdeutschland und anderen Transformationsländern nach 1989* (pp. 186–203). Wiesbaden: Harrassowitz Verlag.

Armstrong, E. & Crage, S. (2006). Movements and memory: The making of the stonewall myth. *American Sociological Review, 71*(1), 724–751.

Baglioni, S., Britta,B., Chabanet D., Lahusen, C. (2008). Transcending marginalization: The mobilization of the unemployed in France, Germany and Italy in a comparative perspective. *Mobilization, 13*(3), 323–335.

Bamberg, M. (1997). Emotion talk (s): The role of perspective in the construction of emotions. In S. Niemeier & R. Dirven (Eds), *The Language of Emotions* (pp. 209–225). Amsterdam, Philadelphia: John Benjamins Publishing Company

Barnes, M. (2015). Survivors, Consumers, or Experts by Experience? Assigned, Chosen, and Contested Identities in the Mental Health Service User Movement. In A. McGarry & J. Jasper (Eds.), *The Identity Dilemma: Social Movements and Collective Identity* (pp. 131–149). Philadelphia: Temple University Press.

Barthes, R. (1975). An introduction to the structural analysis of narrative. *New Literary History, 6*(2), 237–272.

Baumgarten, B. (2016). The children of the carnation revolution? Connections between Portugal's anti-austerity movements and the revolutionary period 1974/1975. *Social Movement Studies, 16*, 51–63.

Bearman, P. S. & Stovel, K. (2000). Becoming a Nazi: A model for narrative networks. *Poetics, 27*, 69–90.

Benford, R. D. (2002). Controlling Narratives and Narratives as Control within Social Movements. In J. E. Davis (Ed.), *Stories of Change: Narrative and Social Movements* (pp. 53–75). New York: SUNY Press.

Bennett, W. L. & Segerberg, A. (2013). *The Logic of Connective Action: Digital Media and The Personalization of Contentious Politics.* New York: Cambridge University Press.

Berger, P. & Luckmann, T. (1991). *The Social Construction of Reality: A Treatise in the Sociology of Knowledge.* London: Penguin Books.

Bernstein, M. C. (1997). Celebration and suppression: The strategic uses of identity by the lesbian and gay movement. *American Journal of Sociology, 103*, 531–565.

Billig, M. (1995). Rhetorical Psychology, Ideological Thinking and Imagining Nationhood. In H. Johnston & B. Klandermans (Eds.), *Social Movements and Culture* (pp. 64–83). Minneapolis: University of Minnesota Press.

Blumer, H. G. (1969). *Symbolic Interactionism.* Englewood Cliffs, NJ: Transaction Publishers.

Bosco, F. J. (2004). Human rights politics and scaled performances of memory: Conflicts among the Madres de Plaza de Mayo in Argentina. *Social & Cultural Geography, 5*(3), 381–402.

Brand, U. (2005). *Gegen-Hegemonie. Perspektiven globalisierungskritischer Strategien.* Hamburg: VSA.

Brown, M. F. (2002). Moving Toward the Light: Self, Other, and the Politics of Experience in New Age Narratives. In J. E. Davis (Ed.), *Stories of change: Narrative and Social Movements* (pp. 101–122). New York: SUNY Press.

Calhoun, C. (1993). "New Social Movements" of the early nineteenth century. *Social Science History, 17*(3), 385–427.

———. (1997). *Nationalism.* Buckingham: Open University Press.

Carr, D. (1986). Narrative and the real world: An argument for continuity. *Historical Theory, 25*(2), 117–131.

Castells, M. (2001). *The Information Age: Economy, Society and Culture: Volume I: The Rise of the Network Society* (2nd edition). Oxford: Blackwell Publishers.

Chatman, S. (1989). *Story and Discourse, Narrative Structure in Fiction and Film.* Cornell: Cornell University Press.

Chesters, G. & Welsh, I. (2004). Rebel colours: 'Framing' in global social movements. *The Sociological Review, 52*(3), 314–335.

Choup, A. M. (2008). The formation and manipulation of collective identity: A framework for analysis. *Social Movement Studies, 7*(2), 191–207.

Císař, O. & Navrátil, J. (2016). Polanyi, political economic opportunity structure and protest: Capitalism and contention in the post-communist Czech Republic. *Social Movement Studies, 16*(1), 82–100.

Cohen, J. L. (1985). Strategy or identity: New theoretical paradigms and contemporary social movements. *Social Research, 52*, 663–716.

Collins, R. (2004). *Interaction Ritual Chains. Princeton, Oxford:* Princeton University Press.

Cornell, S. (2000). That's the Story of Our Life. In P. Spickard & J. Burroughs (Eds.), *We are a People: Narrative and Multiplicity In Constructing Ethnic Identity* (pp. 41–53). Philadelphia: Temple University Press.

Crolley, L. & Hand, D. (2006). *Football and European Identity: Historical Narratives Through the Press.* London & New York: Routledge.

Crowley, J. E. (2009). Fathers' rights groups, domestic violence and political countermobilization. *Social Forces, 88*(2), 723–756.

Cumbers, A., Routledge, P., & Nativel, C. (2008). The entangled geographies of global justice networks. *Progress in Human Geography, 32,* 183–201.

Daphi, P. (2011). Soziale Bewegungen und Kollektive Identität. Forschungsstand und Forschungslücken. *Forschungsjournal Soziale Bewegungen, 24*(4), 13–26.

———. (2013). Collective Identity Across Borders: Bridging Local and Transnational Memories in the Italian and German Global Justice Movements. In L. Cox & C. Flesher Fominaya (Eds.), *Understanding European Movements: New Social Movements, Global Justice Struggles, Anti-Austerity Protest* (pp. 158–171). London: Routledge.

———. (2014a). Movement Space. A Cultural Approach. In B. Baumgarten, P. Daphi & P. Ullrich (Eds.), *Conceptualizing Culture in Social Movement Research* (pp. 165–185). Houndmills: Palgrave Macmillan.

———. (2014b). International Solidarity in the Global Justice Movement: Coping with National and Sectoral Affinities. *Interface: A Journal for and About Social Movements, 6*(2), 164–179.

———. (2017). "Imagine the streets": The spatial dimension of protests' transformative effects and its role in building movement identity. *Political Geography, 56,* 34–43.

Daphi, P. & Rucht, D. (2011). Wir und die anderen. Klärungen und Anwendungen des Konzepts kollektive Identität (Editorial). *Forschungsjournal Soziale Bewegungen, 24*(4), 2–4.

Daro, V. E. (2009). Global justice protest events and the production of knowledge about differences. *McGill Journal of Education/Revue des sciences de l'éducation de McGill, 44*(1), 39–54.

Davis, J. E. (2002). Narrative and Social Movements: The Power of Stories. In J. E. Davis (Ed.), *Stories of Change: Narrative and Social Movements* (pp. 3–30). New York: SUNY Press.

de Fina, A. (2003). *Identity in Narrative. A Study of Immigrant Discourse.* Amsterdam: John Benjamins Publishing Company.

———. (2006). Group identity, narrative and self-presentations. In A. De Fina, D. Schiffrin, & M. Bamberg (Eds.), *Discourse and Identity* (pp. 351–375). Cambridge: Cambridge University Press.

della Porta, D. (1992). Life Histories in the Analysis of Social Movement Activists. In M. Diani & R. Eyerman (Eds.), *Studying Collective Action* (pp. 168–193). London: Sage Publication.

———. (2005a). Multiple Belongings, Tolerant Identities, and the Construction of "Another Politics": Between the European Social Forum and the Local Social Fora.

In D. della Porta & S. G. Tarrow (Eds.), *People, Passions, and Power. Transnational Protest and Global Activism.* Lanham etc.: Rowman & Littlefield.

———. (2005b). Making the polis: social forums and democracy in the global justice movement. *Mobilization: An International Quarterly, 10*(1), 73–94.

———. (2007a). The Global Justice Movement: An Introduction. In D. della Porta (Ed.), *The Global Justice Movement. Cross-National and Transnational Perspectives* (pp. 1–28). Boulder, London: Paradigm Publishers.

———. (2007b). The Global Justice Movement in Context. In D. della Porta (Ed.), *The Global Justice Movement. Cross-National and Transnational Perspectives* (pp. 232–251). Boulder, London: Paradigm Publishers.

———. (2008). Eventful protest, global conflicts. *Distinktion: Scandinavian Journal of Social Theory, 9*(2), 27–56.

———. (2011, June). *Moving up and moving down. Eventful Protest and Organizational Processes.* Paper presented at the conference 'Outcomes of Social Movements and Protest', WZB, Berlin, Germany.

della Porta, D., Andretta, M., Mosca, L., & Reiter, H. (2006). *Globalization from Below: Transnational Activists And Protest Networks. Social Movements, Protest, And Contention: Vol. 26.* Minneapolis: University of Minnesota Press.

della Porta, D. & Diani, M. (2006). *Social Movements: An Introduction.* Oxford Malden Mass.: Blackwell.

della Porta, D. & Mosca, L. (2008). In movimento: 'contamination' in action and the Italian Global Justice Movement. *Global Networks, 7*(1), 1–27.

della Porta, D. & Andretta, M. (2013). Protesting for justice and democracy: Italian Indignados? *Contemporary Italian Politics, 5*(1), 23–37.

Dimond, J. P., Dye, M., LaRose, D., & Bruckman, A. S. (2013). Hollaback!: The Role Of Storytelling Online in a Social Movement Organization. In *Proceedings of the 2013 Conference on Computer Supported Cooperative Work* (pp. 477–490). New York: ACM.

Doerr, N. (2014a). Memory and Culture in Social Movements. In B. Baumgarten, P. Daphi & P. Ullrich (Eds.), *Conceptualizing Culture in Social Movement Research* (pp. 206–226). Houndmills: Palgrave Macmillan.

———. (2014b). The Power of Conflicting Memories in European Transnational Social Movements. In L. Freeman, B. Nienass & R. Daniell (Eds.), *Silence, Screen, and Spectacle: Rethinking Social Memory in the Age of Information* (pp.163–182). New York & Oxford: Berghan.

Domaradzka, A. & Wijkström, F. (2016). Game of the City Re-negotiated: The Polish Urban Re-generation Movement as an Emerging Actor in a Strategic Action Field. *Polish Sociological Review, 195*(3), 291–308.

Downton, J. Jr, & Wehr, P. (1997). *The Persistent Activist: How Peace Commitment Develops and Survives.* Boulder, CO: Westview Press.

Dufour, P. & Giraud, I. (2007). The continuity of transnational solidarities in the world march of women, 2000 and 2005: A collective identity-building approach. *Mobilization: An International Quarterly, 12*(3), 307–322.

Durkheim, E. (1965). *The Elementary Forms of Religious Life.* New York: Free Press.

Eder, K. (2000). *Kulturelle Identität zwischen Tradition und Utopie. Soziale Bewegungen als Ort gesellschaftlicher Lernprozesse.* Frankfurt: Campus Verlag.

————. (2006). Europe's Borders: The narrative construction of the boundaries of Europe. *European Journal of Social Theory, 9*(2), 255–271.

————. (2009). A theory of collective identity making sense of the debate on a 'european identity'. *European Journal of Social Theory, 12*(4), 427–447.

————. (2011). Wie schreiben sich soziale Bewegungen über Zeit fort? Ein narrativer Ansatz. *Forschungsjournal Soziale Bewegungen, 24*(4), 53–72.

Eder, K. & Spohn, W. (Eds.). (2005). *Collective Memory and European Identity: The Effects of Integration and Enlargement.* Aldershot: Ashgate.

Ekiert, G. & Kubik, J. (2001). *Rebellious Civil Society: Popular Protest And Democratic Consolidation in Poland, 1989–1993.* Ann Arbor: University of Michigan Press.

Ekiert, G. & Foa, R. (2011). Civil society weakness in post-communist Europe: A preliminary assessment. *Carlo Alberto Notebooks, 198,* 1–45.

Erll, A. & Rigney, A. (2009). Introduction: Cultural Memory and Its Dynamics. In A. Erll & A. Rigney (Eds.), *Mediation, Remediation, and the Dynamics of Cultural Memory* (pp. 1–14). Berlin & New York: Walter de Gruyter.

Farthing, L. & Kohl, B. (2013). Mobilizing memory: Bolivia's enduring social movements. *Social Movement Studies, 12*(4), 361–376.

Ferree, M. M., Gamson, W., Gerhards, J., & Rucht, D. (2002). *Shaping Abortion Discourse: Democracy and the Public Sphere in Germany and the United States. Communication, Society, and Politics.* Cambridge: Cambridge University Press.

Fine, G. A. (1995). Public Narration and Group Culture: Discerning Discourse in Social Movements. In H. Johnston & B. Klandermans (Eds.), *Social Movements and Culture* (pp. 127–143). Minneapolis: University of Minnesota Press.

————. (2002). The Storied Group: Social Movements as 'Bundles of Narratives'. In J. E. Davis (Ed.), *Stories of Change: Narrative and Social Movements* (pp. 229–245). New York: SUNY Press.

Finelli, P. (2003). 'Un'idea partecipativa della politica'. Strutture organizzative e modelli di democrazia in Attac Italia. In P. Ceri (Ed.), *La democrazia dei movimenti: come decidono i noglobal* (pp. 31–56). Soveria Mannelli: Rubbettino.

Flesher Fominaya, C. 2007). The role of humour in the process of collective identity formation in autonomous social movement groups in contemporary Madrid. *International Review of Social History, 52,* 243–258.

————. (2010a). Collective identity in social movements: Central concepts and debates. *Sociology Compass, 4*(6), 393–404.

————. (2010b). Creating cohesion from diversity: The challenge of collective identity formation in the global justice movement. *Sociological Inquiry, 80,* 377–404.

————. (2014). Movement Culture as Habit(us): Resistance to Change in the Routinized Practices of Resistance. In B. Baumgarten, P. Daphi & P. Ullrich (Eds.), *Conceptualizing Culture in Social Movement Research* (pp. 186–205). Houndmills: Palgrave Macmillan.

————. (2015). Debunking spontaneity: Spain's 15-M/Indignados as autonomous movement. *Social Movement Studies, 14,* 142–163.

————. (2016). Unintended consequences: The negative impact of e-mail use on participation and collective identity in two 'horizontal' social movement groups. *European Political Science Review, 8*(1), 95–122.

————. (2017). European anti-austerity and pro-democracy protests in the wake of the global financial crisis. *Social Movement Studies*, *16*(1), 1–20.

Franzosi, R. (1998). Narrative analysis – or why (And How) sociologists should be interested in narrative. *Annual Review of Sociology*, *24*, 517–554.

Fukuyama, F. (1992). The End of History and the Last Man. London: Penguin.

Gamson, J. (1997). Messages of exclusion: Gender, movements, and symbolic boundaries. *Gender & Society*, *11*(2), 178–199.

Gamson, W. (1992). The Social Psychology of Collective Action. In A. D. Morris & C. M. C. Mueller (Eds.), *Frontiers in Social Movement Theory* (pp. 53–76). New Haven CT: Yale University Press.

Gerbaudo, P. (2016). The indignant citizen: Anti-austerity movements in southern Europe and the anti-oligarchic reclaiming of citizenship. *Social Movement Studies*, *16*, 36–50.

Gerbaudo, P. & Treré, E. (2015). In search of the 'we' of social media activism: Introduction to the special issue on social media and protest identities. *Information, Communication & Society*, *18*(8), 865–871.

Gerhards, J. & Rucht, D. (1992). Mesomobilization: Organizing and framing in two protest campaigns in West Germany. *The American Journal of Sociology*, *98*(3), 555–596.

Goffman, E. (1974). *Frame Analysis: An Essay on the Organization of Experience*. Boston: Northeastern University Press.

Gongaware, T. B. (2011). Keying the past to the present: Collective memories and continuity in collective identity change. *Social Movement Studies*, *10*, 39–54.

Goodwin, J., Jasper, J. M., & Polletta, F. (2008). Emotional Dimensions of Social Movements. In D. A. Snow, S. H. Soule & H. Kriesi (Eds.), *The Blackwell Companion to Social Movements* (2nd edition, pp. 413–432). Malden etc., MA: Blackwell.

Greimas, A. (1970). *Du Sens*. Paris: Seuil.

Halbwachs, M. (1980a [1950]). *The Collective Memory*. New York: Harper & Row.

————. (1966 [1925]). *Das Gedächtnis und seine sozialen Bedingungen*. Berlin: Luchterhand.

Harris, F. C. (2006). It takes a tragedy to arouse them: Collective memory and collective action during the civil rights movement. *Social Movement Studies*, *5*(1), 19–43.

Harris, C. B., Paterson, H. M., & Kemp, R. I. (2008). Collaborative recall and collective memory: What happens when we remember together? *Memory*, *16*(3), 213–230.

Hart, J. (1992). Cracking the code: Narrative and political mobilization in the Greek resistance. *Social Science History*, *16*(4), 630–668.

Haug, C. (2013). Organizing spaces: Meeting arenas as a social movement infrastructure between organization, network, and institution. *Organization Studies*, *34*(5–6), 705–732.

Haug, C., Teune, S., & Yang, M. (2007). Lokale Sozialforen in Deutschland. In L. Schwalb & H. Walk (Eds.), *Local Governance—mehr Transparenz und Bürgernähe?* (pp. 206–227). VS Verlag für Sozialwissenschaften.

Haunss, S. (2004). *Identität in Bewegung: Prozesse kollektiver Identität bei den Autonomen und in der Schwulenbewegung.* Wiesbaden: VS Verlag für Sozialwissenschaften.

———. (2011). Kollektive Identität, soziale Bewegungen und Szenen. *Forschungsjournal Soziale Bewegungen, 24*(4), 41–52.

Holland, D., Fox, G., & Daro, V. (2008). Social movements and collective identity. A decentred and dialogic view. *Anthropological Quarterly, 81*(1), 95–126.

Hunt, S. A., Benford, R. D., & Snow, D. A. (1994). Identity Fields: Framing Processes and the Social Construction of Movement Identities. In E. Laraña, H. Johnston, & J. R. Gusfield (Eds.), *New Social Movements: From Ideology to Identity.* Philadelphia: Temple University Press.

Hunt, S. A. & Benford, R. D. (1994). Identity talk in the peace and justice movement. *Journal of Contemporary Ethnography, 22*(4), 488–517.

———. (2008). Collective Identity, Solidarity, and Commitment. In D. A. Snow, S. H. Soule & H. Kriesi (Eds.), *The Blackwell Companion to Social Movements* (2nd edition, pp. 433–457). Malden etc., MA: Blackwell.

Hutter, S. (2014). *Protesting Culture and Economics in Western Europe.* Minneapolis: University of Minnesota Press.

Jacobs, R. N. (2002). The Narrative Integration of Personal and Collective Identity in Social Movements. In M. C. Green, J. J. Strange, T. C. Brock (Eds.), *Narrative Impact: Social and Cognitive Foundations* (pp. 205–228). Mahwah, NJ: Lawrence Erlbaum.

Jacobs, R. N. & Smith, P. (1997). Romance, irony, and solidarity. *Sociological Theory, 15*(1), 60–80.

Jansen, R. S. (2007). Resurrection and appropriation: Reputational trajectories, memory work, and the political use of historical figures. *American Journal of Sociology, 112*(4), 953–1007.

Jasper, J. M. (1997). *The Art of Moral Protest: Culture, Biography, and Creativity in Social Movements.* Chicago: University of Chicago Press.

———. (1998). The emotions of protest: The affective and reactive emotions in and around social movements. *Sociological Forum, 13*(3), 397–424.

———. (2014). Feeling-Thinking: Emotions as Central to Culture. In B. Baumgarten, P. Daphi & P. Ullrich (Eds.), *Conceptualizing Culture in Social Movement Research* (pp. 23–44). Houndmills: Palgrave Macmillan.

Jasper, J. & McGarry, A. (2015). Introduction: The Identity Dilemma, Social Movements, and Contested Identity. In A. McGarry & J. Jasper (Eds.), *The Identity Dilemma: Social Movements and Collective Identity* (pp. 1–17). Philadelphia: Temple University Press.

Jasper, J., Tramontano, M., & McGarry, A. (2015). Scholarly Research on Collective Identity. In A. McGarry & J. Jasper (Eds.), *The Identity Dilemma: Social Movements and Collective Identity* (pp. 18–43). Philadelphia: Temple University Press.

Jenkins, J. C. (1983). Resource mobilization theory and the study of social movements. *Annual Review of Sociology, 9*, 527–553.

Johnston, H., Laraña, E., & Gusfield, J. R. (1994). Identities, Grievances, and New Social Movements. In E. Laraña, H. Johnston, & J. R. Gusfield (Eds.), *New Social*

Movements: From Ideology to Identity (pp. 3–35). Philadelphia: Temple University Press.

Juris, J. S. (2005). Violence performed and imagined militant action, the Black Bloc and the mass media in Genoa. *Critique of Anthropology, 25*(4), 413–432.

———. (2008a). *Networking Futures: The Movements Against Corporate Globalization.* Durham & London: Duke University Press.

———. (2008b). Performing politics: Image, embodiment, and affective solidarity during anti-corporate globalization protests. *Ethnography, 9*(1), 61–97.

Kane, A. (2000). Narratives of nationalism: constructing Irish national identity during the land war, 1879–1882. *National Identities, 2*, 245–264.

Kern, T. & Nam, S. H. (2013). From 'corruption' to 'democracy': Cultural values, mobilization, and the collective identity of the occupy movement. *Journal of Civil Society, 9*(2), 196–211.

King, D. (2004). Operationalizing Melucci: Metamorphosis and passion in the negotiation of activists' multiple identities. *Mobilization: An International Quarterly, 9*(1), 73–92.

Klandermans, B. (2000). Identity and protest: How group identification helps to overcome collective action dilemmas. In M. van Vugt, T. Snyder, T. R. Tyler, & A. Biehl (Eds.), *Collective Helping in Modern Society* (pp.162–183). London: Routledge.

Kleres, J. (2011). Emotions and narrative analysis: A methodological approach. *Journal for the Theory of Social Behaviour, 41*(2), 182–202.

Kolb, F. (2004). Mass Media and the Making of ATTAC Germany. In D. della Porta & S. G. Tarrow (Eds.), *Transnational Protest and Global Activism* (pp. 95–120). Lanham.: Rowman & Littlefield.

Kurzman, C. (2008). Introduction: Meaning-making in social movements. *Anthropological Quarterly, 81*(1), 5–15.

Labov, W. & Waleztky, J. (1967). Narrative Analysis: Oral Versions of Personal Experience. In J. Helm (Ed.), *Essays on the Verbal and Virtual Arts; Proceedings of the 1966 Annual Spring Meeting of the American Ethnological Society* (pp. 12–44). Seattle: University of Washington Press.

Leach, D. & Haunss, S. (2008). Scenes and Social Movements. In H. Johnston (Ed.), *Culture, Social Movements, and Protest* (pp. 255–276). Aldershot Hants: Ashgate.

Lehnert, W. & Vine, E. (1987). The role of affect in narrative structure. *Cognition and Emotion, 1*(3), 299–322.

Levi-Strauss, C. (1963). *The Structural Analysis of Myth.* New York: Basic Books.

Loseke, D. R. (2007). The study of identity as cultural, institutional, organizational, and personal narratives: Theoretical and empirical integrations. *The Sociological Quarterly, 48*(4), 661–688.

MacIntyre, A. (1981). *After Virtue: A Study in Moral Theory.* Durham, NC: Duke University Press.

Maeckelbergh, M. (2012). Horizontal democracy now: From alterglobalization to occupation. *Interface: A Journal for and About Social Movements, 4*(1), 207–234.

Maiba, H. (2005). Grassroots transnational social movement activism: The case of peoples' global action. *Sociological Focus, 38*, 41–63.

McAdam, D. & Sewell, W. H. (2001). It's about Time: Temporality in the Study of Social Movements and Revolutions. In R. Aminzade, D. McAdam, E. Perry, W. H. Sewell, S. Tarrow & C. Tilly (Eds.), *Silence and Voice in the Study of Contentious Politics* (pp. 89–125). Cambridge, New York: Cambridge University Press.

McCright, A. M. & Dunlap, R. E. (2015). Comparing two measures of social movement identity: The environmental movement as an example. *Social Science Quarterly, 96*(2), 400–416.

McDonald, K. (2002). From solidarity to fluidarity: Social movements beyond 'collective identity' the case of globalization conflicts. *Social Movement Studies, 1*(2), 109–128.

Melucci, A. (1989). *Nomads of the Present: Social Movements and Individual Needs in Contemporary Society.* Philadelphia, PA: Temple University Press.

———. (1996). *Challenging Codes: Collective Action in the Information Age.* New York: Cambridge University Press.

Membretti, A. & Mudu, P. (2013). Where Global Meets Local: Italian Social Centres and the Alterglobalization Movement. In C. Flesher Fominaya & L. Cox (Eds.), *The European Social Movement Experience: Rethinking 'new social movements', Historicising the Alterglobalisation Movement and Understanding the New Wave of Protest* (pp.76 – 93). London/New York: Routledge.

Navrátil, J. (2010). Between the spillover and the spillout: Tracing the evolution of the Czech global justice movement. *Czech Sociological Review, 6*(1), 913–944.

Nepstad, S. E. (2001). Creating transnational solidarity: The use of narrative in the U.S.-Central America Peace Movement. *Mobilization: An International Journal, 6*(1), 21–36.Nip, J. Y. M. (2004). The Queer Sisters and its Electronic Bulletin Board: A Study of the Internet for Social Movement Mobilization. *Information, Communication & Society, 7*(1), 23–49. Niwot, M. (2011). Narrating Genoa: Documentaries of the Italian G8 protests of 2001 and the persistence and politics of memory. *History & Memory, 23*(2), 66–89.

Niwot, M. (2011). Narrating Genoa: Documentaries of the Italian G8 protests of 2001 and the persistence and politics of memory. *History & Memory, 23*(2), 66-89.

Olick, J. K. (1999). Collective memory: The two cultures. *Sociological Theory, 17*(3), 333–348.

Olick J. K. & Levy, D. (1997). Collective memory and cultural constraint: Holocaust myth and rationality in German politics. *Amercian Sociological Review, 62,* 921–936.

Ost, D. (2005). *The Defeat of Solidarity: Anger and Politics in Postcommunist Europe.* Cornell: Cornell University Press.

Owens L. (2009). *Cracking Under Pressure: Narrating the Decline of the Amsterdam Squatters' Movements.* Amsterdam: Amsterdam University Press.

Passy, F. & Giugni, M. (2000). Life-spheres, networks, and sustained participation in social movements: A phenomenological approach to political commitment. *Sociological Forum, 15*(1), 117–144.

Payerhin, M. & Ernesto Zirakzadeh, C. (2006). On movement frames and negotiated identities: The case of Poland's first solidarity congress. *Social Movement Studies, 5*(2), 91–115.

Petrova, T. & Tarrow, S. (2007). Transactional and participatory activism in the emerging European polity the puzzle of East-Central Europe. *Comparative Political Studies, 40*(1), 74–94.

Piotrowski, G. (2009). Civil society, Un-civil society and the social movements in central and Eastern Europe. *Interface: A Journal for and About Social Movements, 1*(2), 166–189.

———. (2010). *Alterglobalism in Postsocialism: A Study of Central and Eastern European Actors.* PhD Thesis, European University Institute, Florence.

———. (2013). Social movement or subculture? Alterglobalists in Central and Eastern Europe. *Interface: A Journal for and About Social Movements, 5*(2), 399–421.

———. (2017). *In the Shadow of the Iron Curtain. Central and Eastern European Alterglobalists.* Frankfurt: Peter Lang.

Polletta, F. (1998a). Contending stories: Narrative in social movements. *Qualitative Sociology, 21*, 419–446.

———. (1998b). 'It Was like a Fever …': Narrative and identity in social protest. *Social Problems, 45*(2), 137–159.

———. (2006). *It Was Like a Fever: Storytelling in Protest and Politics.* Chicago: University of Chicago Press.

———. (2008). Culture and movements. *The Annals of the American Academy, 619*, 78–96.

Polletta, F. & Jasper, J. M. (2001). Collective identity and social movements. *Annual Review of Sociology, 27*, 283–305.

Polletta, F., Chen, P., Garnder, B., & Motes, A. (2011). The sociology of storytelling. *Annual Review of Sociology, 37*(1), 109–130.

Polletta, F., Trigoso, M., Adams, B., & Ebner, A. (2013). The limits of plot: Accounting for how women interpret stories of sexual assault. *American Journal of Cultural Sociology, 1*(3), 289–320.

Polkinghorne, D. (1988). *Narrative Knowing and the Human Sciences.* Albany: State University N.Y. Press.

Prins, J., van Stekelenburg, J., Polletta, F., & Klandermans, B. (2013). Telling the collective story? Moroccan-Dutch young adults' negotiation of a collective identity through storytelling. *Qualitative Sociology, 36*(1), 81–99.

Propp, V. (1968). *Morphology of the Folktale.* Dallas: University of Texas Press.

Rae, G. (2008). The birth of a new intellectual left in Poland? *Debatte, 16*(3), 253–272.

Rappaport, J. (1993). Narrative studies, personal stories, and identity transformation in the mutual help context. *The Journal of Applied Behavioral Science, 29*(2), 239–256.

Reiter, H., Andretta, M., della Porta, D., & Mosca, L. (2007). The Global Justice Movement in Italy. In D. della Porta (Ed.), *The Global Justice Movement: Cross-National and Transnational Perspectives* (pp. 52–78). Boulder, London: Paradigm Publishers.

Rice, J. S. (2002). 'Getting our Histories Straight': Culture, Narrative, and Identity in the Self-Help Movement. In J. E. Davis (Ed.), *Stories of Change: Narrative and Social Movements* (pp. 79–100). New York: SUNY Press.

Ricoeur, P. (1984). *Time and Narrative.* Chicago: University of Chicago Press.

———. (1991). Myths as a Bearer of Possible Worlds. In M. Valdes (Ed.), *Reflections & Imagination* (pp. 482–490). New York: Harvester.

Roth, R. & Rucht, D. (Eds.). (2008). *Die sozialen Bewegungen in Deutschland seit 1945: ein Handbuch*. Frankfurt: Campus Verlag.

Rothenberg, B. (2002). Movement Advocates as Battered Women's Storytellers. In J. E. Davis (Ed.), *Stories of Change: Narrative and Social Movements* (pp. 195–214). New York: SUNY Press.

Rucht, D. (1995). Kollektive Identität: Konzeptionelle Überlegungen zu einem Desiderat der Bewegungsforschung. *Forschungsjournal, 8*(1), 9–23.

———. (2002). Herausforderungen für die globalisierungskritischen Bewegungen. *Forschungsjournal Soziale Bewegungen, 15*(1), 16–21.

———. (2003). Die Friedensdemonstranten–Wer sind sie, wofür stehen sie. *Forschungsjournal Neue Soziale Bewegungen, 16*(2), 10–13.

———. (2011). The strength of weak identities. *Forschungsjournal Soziale Bewegungen, 24*(4), 73–84.

Rucht, D., Teune, S., & Yang, M. (2007). The Global Justice Movements in Germany. In D. della Porta (Ed.), *The Global Justice Movement: Cross-National and Transnational Perspectives*. Boulder, London: Paradigm Publishers.

Rucht, D. & Roth, R. (2008). Globalisierungskritische Netzwerke, Kampagnen und Bewegungen. In R. Roth & D. Rucht (Eds.), *Die sozialen Bewegungen in Deutschland seit 1945. Ein Handbuch* (pp. 493–512). Frankfurt/Main: Campus Verlag.

Russo, C. (2014). Allies forging collective identity: Embodiment and emotions on the migrant trail. *Mobilization: An International Quarterly, 19*(1), 67–82.

Sewell, William H. (1996). Three Temporalities: Toward an Eventful Sociology. In McDonald, Terence J. (Eds.), *The Historic Turn in the Human Sciences* (pp. 245–280). Ann Arbor: University of Michigan Press.

Sewell, W. H. Jr. & McAdam, D. (2001). It's About Time: Temporality in the Study of Social Movements and Revolutions. In R. Aminzade, D. McAdam, E. Perry, W. H. Sewell, S. Tarrow & C. Tilly (Eds.), *Silence and Voice in the Study of Contentious Politics* (pp. 89–125). Cambridge, New York: Cambridge University Press.

Shields, S. (2012). Opposing neoliberalism? Poland's renewed populism and post-communist transition. *Third World Quarterly, 33*(2), 359–381.

Simon, B. & Klandermans, B. (2001). Politicized collective identity: A social psychological analysis. *American Psychologist, 56*(4), 319–331.

Smith, A. D. (1999). *Myths and Memories of the Nation*. Oxford: Oxford University Press.

Smith, J. (2001). Globalizing resistance: The Battle of Seattle and the feature of social movements. *Mobilization: An International Journal, 6*(1), 1–20.

Smith, T. (2007). Narrative boundaries and the dynamics of ethnic conflict and conciliation. *Poetics, 35*, 22–46.

Snow, D. A., Rocheford, E. B., & Benford, R. D. (1986). Frame alignment processes, micromobilzation, and movement participation. *American Sociological Review, 51*, 464–481.

Snow, D. A. & Anderson, L. (1987). Identity work among the homeless: The verbal construction and avowal of personal identities. *American Journal of Sociology, 92*(6), 1336–1371.

Snow, D. A. & Benford, R. D. (1988). Ideology, frame resonance, and participant mobilization. Int. Soc. Mov. Res. *International Social Movement Research, 1*, 197–218.

———. (1992). Master Frames and Cycles of Protest. In A. D. Morris & C. M. C. Mueller (Eds.), *Frontiers in Social Movement Theory* (pp. 133–155). New Haven, CT: Yale University Press.

Snow, D. A. & McAdam, D. (2000). Identity Work Processes in the Context of Social Movements: Clarifying the Identity/Movement Nexus. In S. Stryker, T. J. Owens, & R. W. White (Eds.), *Self, Identity, and Social Movements*. Minneapolis: University of Minnesota Press.

Somers, M. R. (1992). Narrativity, narrative identity, and social action: Rethinking english working-class formation. *Social Science History, 16*(4), 591–630.

———. (1994). The narrative constitution of identity: A relational and network approach. *Theory and Society, 23*, 605–649.

———. (1995). Narrating and naturalizing civil society and citizenship theory: The place of political culture and the public sphere. *Sociological Theory, 13*(3), 229–274.

Steinmetz, G. (1992). Reflections on the role of social narratives in working-class formation: Narrative theory and the social sciences. *Social Science History, 16*, 489–515.

Stekelenburg, J. (2014). Going all the way: Politicizing, polarizing, and radicalizing identity offline and online. *Sociology Compass, 8*(5), 540–555.

Steward G. A. Jr., Shriver, T. E., & Chasteen, A. L. (2002). Participant narratives and collective identity in a metaphysical movement. *Sociological Spectrum, 22*(1), 107–135.

Tarrow, S. (1992). Mentalities, Political Cultures, and Collective Action Frames: Constructing Meanings through Action. In A. D. Morris & C. M. C. Mueller (Eds.), *Frontiers in Social Movement Theory* (pp. 174–202). New Haven, CT: Yale University Press.

———. (1998). *Power in Movement*. Cambridge: Cambridge University Press.

———. (2001). Transnational politics: Contention and institutions in international politics. *Annual Review of Political Science, 4*(1), 1–20.

———. (2005). *The New Transnational Activism*. Cambridge etc.: Cambridge University Press.

Taylor, V. (1989). Social movement continuity: The women's movement in abeyance. *American Sociological Review, 54*(5), 761–775.

Taylor, V. & Whittier, N. (1992). Collective Identity in Social Movement Communities: Lesbian Feminist Mobilization. In A. D. Morris & C. M. C. Mueller (Eds.), *Frontiers in Social Movement Theory*. New Haven, CT: Yale University Press.

Taylor, V. & Van Dyke, N. (2008). Get up, Stand up: Tactical Repertoires of Social Movements. In D. A. Snow, S. A. Soule & H. Kriesi (Eds.), *The Blackwell Companion to Social Movements* (pp. 262–293).Oxford: Blackwell.

Taylor, V. & Leitz, L. (2010). Emotions and Identity in Self-Help Movements. In J. C. Banaszak-Holl, S. Levitsky & M. N. Zald (Eds.) , *Social Movements and the Transformation of American Health Care* (pp. 266–283). Oxford: Oxford University Press.

Teune, S. (2012). *Corridors of Action: Protest Rationalities and the Channeling of Anti-Summit Repertoires*. PhD Thesis, Freie Universität Berlin, Berlin.

Tilly, C. (1995). *Popular Contention in Great Britain, 1758–1834*. Cambridge: Harvard University Press.

———. (2002). *Stories, Identities, and Political Change*. Lanham.: Rowman & Littlefield.

Todorov, T. & Weinstein, A. (1969). Structural analysis of narrative. *Novel: A Forum on Fiction, 3*(1), 70–76.

Touraine, A. (1977). *The Self-Production of Society*. Chicago: University of Chicago Press.

———. (1981). *The Voice and the Eye: An Analysis of Social Movements*. Cambridge: Cambridge University Press.

Tucker, C. (2013). Using social network analysis and framing to assess collective identity in the genetic engineering resistance movement of Aotearoa New Zealand. *Social Movement Studies, 12*(1), 81–95.

Uggla, F. (2006). Between globalism and pragmatism: ATTAC in France, Germany, and Sweden. *Mobilization: An International Quarterly, 11*, 51–66.

Vicari, S. (2015). The interpretive dimension of transformative events: Outrage management and collective action framing after the 2001 Anti-G8 Summit in Genoa. *Social Movement Studies, 14*(5), 596–614.

Veltri, F. (2003). 'Non si chiama delega, si chiama fiducia'. La sfida organizzativa della Rete di Lilliput. In P. Ceri (Ed.), *La democrazia dei movimenti: come decidono i noglobal* (pp. 3–30). Soveria Mannelli: Rubbettino.

Wall, M. A. (2005). Social movements and email: Expressions of online identity in the globalization process. *New Media and Society, 9*(2), 258–277.

White, H. C. (1981). The Value of Narrativity in the Representation of Reality. In W. Mitchell (Ed.), *On Narrative* (pp. 1–23). Chicago, London: University of Chicago Press.

Whittier, N. (1997). Political generations, micro-cohorts, and the transformation of social movements. *American Sociological Review, 62*(5), 760–778.

Wood, L. J. (2005). Bridging the Chasms: The Case of People's Global Action. In J. Bandy & J. Smith (Eds.), *Coalitions Across Borders: Trans-national Protest and the Neoliberal Order* (pp. 95–117). Lanham etc.: Rowman & Littlefield.

Wood, L. J. (2012). *Direct Action, Deliberation, and Diffusion: Collective Action After the WTO Protests in Seattle*. Cambridge: Cambridge University Press.

Zamponi, L. (2015). *Memory in Action: Mediatised Public Memory and the Symbolic Construction of Conflict in Student Movements*. PhD Thesis, European University Institute, Florence.

Zamponi, L. & Daphi, P. (2014). Breaks and Continuities in and Between Cycles of Protest. Memories and Legacies of the Global Justice Movement in the Context of Anti-austerity Mobilisations. In D. della Porta & A. Mattoni (Eds.), *Spreading Protests: Social Movements in Times of Crisis* (pp. 193–226). Essex: ECPR-Press.

Zerubavel, E. (1995). *Recovered Roots: Collective Memory and the Making of Israeli National Tradition*. Chicago: University of Chicago Press.

———. (1996). Social memories: Steps to a sociology of the past. *Qualitative Sociology, 19*(3), 283–299.

Cited GJM Documents[1]

DOCUMENTS ITALY (DOC-IT)

Document 1   Anonymous (2000). *After S26 – ya basta interview. Changing the World (One Bridge At A Time)? Ya Basta after Prague* https://www.nadir.org/nadir/initiativ/agp/s26/praga/bianche.htm

Document 2   Federico Mariani cited in an article by Jess Ramirez Cuevas (2000): *The Body As a Weapon for Civil Disobedience. La Jornada*, October 15, 2000. Available in English translation at https://www.nadir.org/nadir/initiativ/agp/s26/praga/bianche.htm

Document 3   Rete No Global (2001). Dalle resistenze locali ai movimenti globali. In Rete No Global (Eds.), *Zona Rossa: le "quattro giornate di Napoli" contro il Global forum* (pp.12–20). Rome: DeriveApprodi.

Document 4   Rete No Global (2001). Appello per il contro-Global forum, Napoli, 15–17 Marzo 2001. In Rete No Global (Eds.), *Zona Rossa: le "quattro giornate di Napoli" contro il Global forum* (pp. 37–39). DeriveApprodi: Roma.

Document 5   Casarini, L. & Callinicos, A. (2001). Tute Bianchi and the Socialist Workers Party. *How does the anti-capitalist movement face up to the challenges of war and state repression? Luca Casarini and Alex Callinicos discuss the issues. Socialist Review, 258.* December 2001, available at https://www.nadir.org/nadir/initiativ/agp/free/tute/tutebiancheswp.htm

Document 6   Attac Italia (2001). ATTAC a Roma l'8/9/10 Novembre: contro la guerra contro il WTO. *Granello Di Sabbia, 11.* 1–2.

Document 7   Attac Roma (2001). Partecipiamo Tutti e Tutte alla Manifestazione Nazionale Del 10 Novembre a Roma e al Forum. *Granello Di Sabbia, 11.* 2–3.

Document 8   Chiesa, Giulietto (2002). Dopo Genoa. Riflessioni preliminary. In Milano Social Forum (Eds.), *Genova – Il Libro Bianco* (pp. 202–208).

Document 9   Bersani, Marco (2002). Dopo Porto Alegre. In Milano Social Forum (Eds.), *Genova – Il Libro Bianco* (pp. 214–217).

Document 10   Caminiti, Lanfranco (2002). Come è scialbo il documento di Porto Alegre! *Granello Di Sabbia, 33.* 6–8.

Document 11   Nevola, Don Massimo (2002). Sentinella, quanto resta della notte? (Isaia 21,11). A margine di Porto Alegre e di Plaza de Mayo. *Granello di Sabbia, 33.* 9–11.

Document 12   Muhlbauer, Luciano (2002). Dopo Barcellona e Roma: mobilitazione europea contro la precarietà globale. *Granello Di Sabbia, 41.* 4–5.

Document 13   Forum Sociale Genovese (2002). Genova, le nostre ragioni. *Granello Di Sabbia, 60.* 3–5.

Document 14   Attac Italia (2002). Editorial. *Granello Di Sabbia, 63.* 1.

Document 15   Riolo, Girgio (2002). La guerra è la politica. Alcune note sparse. *Granello di Sabbia, 64.* 2–5.

Document 16   Minni, Sergio (2002). Firenze: di chi è la "colpa" della tranquillità del corteo? *Granello di Sabbia, 72.* 2–3.

Document 17   Cannavò, Salvatore (2002). Impressioni da Firenze. *Granello di Sabbia, 73.* 2–4.

Document 18   Bifo (2002). Satori a Firenze: l'evoluzione zen del movimento. *Granello di Sabbia, 73.* 6–7.

DOCUMENTS GERMANY (DOC-DE)

Document 1   Böhnel, Max (1999). Teamsters and Turtles. "Unamerikanische Umtriebe" in Seattle. *Analyse & Kritik, 433.* https://www.akweb.de/ak_s/ak433/35.htm

Document 2   Herndlhofer, Martin (2000). Krieg mit anderen Mitteln. *Zeitschrift der deutschen Sektion der internationalen katholischen Friedensbewegung Pax Christi, 2.* 4–5.

Document 3   Herndlhofer, Martin (2001). Pax Christi und attac: ein Zwischenruf. *Zeitschrift der deutschen Sektion der internationalen katholischen Friedensbewegung Pax Christi, 4.* 17..

Document 4   Anti-WTO Koordination (2001). Auf nach Davos! Internationale Gegenmobilisierung gegen das Weltwirtschaftsforum. *Analyse & Kritik, 446.* https://www.akweb.de/ak_s/ak446/07.htm

Document 5   Rätz, Werner (2001). "Pfui, Reformismus!"? Warum *attac* für die radikale Linke wichtig ist. *Analyse & Kritik, 456.* https://www.akweb.de/ak_s/ak456/22.htm

Document 6   Christine Buchholz cited in an article by Harald Schumann und Gabor Steingart (2001). *Globalisierung von unten.* Spiegel Online, July 30, 2001. http://www.spiegel.de/politik/ deutschland/spiegel-gespraech-globalisierung-von-unten -a-147720.html

Document 7   Stanicic, Sascha (2002). Einleitung. In Sozialistische Alternative (Ed.). *Die Ideen von Seattle und Genua. Eine Kritik der Kritiker* (pp. 3–4). Berlin: SAV

Document 8   Attac Deutschland/Österreich (2003). Editorial. *Sand im Getriebe, 18.* 1.

Document 9   Wahl, Peter (2003). In Den Zwickmühlen des Erfolgs. Eine Bilanz des Dritten Weltsozialforums in Porto Alegre. *Sand im Getriebe, 18.* 16–17.

Document 10   Bruns, Theo (2003). Radikal global – eine Einleitung. In M. Hierlmeier, A. Schudy, M. Wissen (Eds.). *Radikal Global. Bausteine für eine internationalistische Linke* (pp. 3–9). Berlin: Assoziation A Verlag

Document 11   Seibert, Thomas (2003). The People of Genova. Plädoyer für eine post-avantgardistische Linke. In M. Hierlmeier, A. Schudy, M. Wissen (Eds.). *Radikal Global. Bausteine für eine internationalistische Linke* (pp. 57–70). Berlin: Assoziation A Verlag.

DOCUMENTS POLAND (DOC-PL)

Document 1   Grzegorczyk, Jakub (2001, July). *Czy rzeczywiście nie ma alternatywy?* http://www.attac.pl/?dzial=128&typ=2&kat=12 8&lg=pl&id=98

Document 2   Markowski, Konrad (2001a, September). *Złodzieje z lepszych sfer.* http://www.attac.pl/?lg=pl&kat=2&dzial=128&typ=2& id=75

Document 3   Markowski, Konrad (2001b, September). *Po Genui – nic nie będzie już jak przedtem.* http://www.attac.pl/?dzial=128&typ =2&kat=128&lg=pl&id=95

Document 4   Grzegorczyk, Jakub (2001b, October). *Nie wszystko na sprzedaż.* http://www.attac.pl/?dzial=128&typ=2&kat=128&l g=pl&id=101

Document 5   Muskat, Maciej (2001a, October). *Dlatego ATTAC zaczął od podatku Tobina.* http://www.attac.pl/?dzial=128&typ=2&kat= 128&lg=pl&id=77

Document 6   Muskat, Maciej (2001b, November). *Czwarte spotkanie ministerialne Światowej Organizacji Handlu (WTO) w Doha (KATAR).* http://www.attac.pl/?dzial=128&typ=2&kat=128&lg=pl&id=190

Document 7   Dariusz Zalega (2001, November). *Wyjść z pułapki zadłużeniowej.* http://www.attac.pl/?lg=pl&kat=2&dzial=128&typ=2&id=73

Document 8   Ciszewski , Piotr (2002, November). *Inna Europa jest możliwa.* http://www.attac.pl/?dzial=128&typ=2&kat=128&lg=pl&id=147

Document 9   Zaremba, Daniel (2004, March). *Trzy antyglobalizmy.* http://www.attac.pl/?dzial=128&typ=2&kat=128&lg=pl&id=112

Document 10 Chmielewski, Adam (2004, April). *Stawić czoło globalizacji. Interviewed by Maciej Muskat.* http://www.attac.pl/?dzial=128&typ=2&kat=128&lg=pl&id=61

Document 11 Marcin Starnawski (2005, January). *Okupacja umysłów.* http://www.attac.pl/?lg=pl&kat=2&dzial=128&typ=2&id=24

INTERNATIONAL DOCUMENTS (DOC-INT)

Document 1   Peoples' Global Action (1998). Global Days of Action against "Free" Trade and the WTO – May 1998, Geneva. *PGA Bulletin 2.* https://www.nadir.org/nadir/initiativ/agp/en/pgainfos/bulletin2/bulletin2b.html#ActionDays.

Document 2   Ramonet, I. (1999). *A new totalitarianism.* Foreign Policy, (116), 116–121.

Document 3   Indymedia France (2000). *Sintezi delle notizie d'indimedia da Nizza.* https://www.nadir.org/nadir/initiativ/agp/free/nice/sintezi.htm.

Document 4   Lusson, Julien (2001). Di fronte all'FMI, alla Banca Mondiale e all'OMC : giustizia mondiale!. *Granello di Sabbia,3.* 5–6.

Document 5   Aguiton, Christophe (2002). Die größte Demonstration gegen die liberale Globalisierung, die es je gegeben hat. *Sand im Getriebe, 7.* 2–4.

Document 6   Starhawk (2001). Solo la poesia può salvarci dopo l'11 Settembre. *Granello di Sabbia, 19.* 1–7.

Document 7   Chomsky, Noam (2002). *A World Without War.* Speech delivered at the World Social Forum, Porto Alegre, January 31, 2002, https://chomsky.info/200202.

Document 8   George, Susan (2002). Wir sind nicht mehr in der Defensive. In B. Cassen, S: George, H.E. Richter, & J. Ziegler (Eds.), *Eine andere Welt ist möglich!* (pp. 142–150). Hamburg: VSA-Verlag.

Document 9   Notes from Nowhere (2002). One No and many Yeses. An introduction. In Notes from Nowhere (Eds.), *Notes from everywhere*. http://artactivism.gn.apc.org/stories/oneno.htm

Document 10   Notes from Nowhere (2003). Emergence: an irresistible global uprising. In Notes from Nowhere (Eds.), *We are everywhere: the irresistible rise of global anticapitalism* (pp. 19–29). London/New York: Verso.

Document 11   Notes from Nowhere (2003). Networks: the ecology of the movements. In Notes from Nowhere (Eds.). *We are everywhere: the irresistible rise of global anticapitalism* (pp. 63–73). London/New York: Verso.

Document 12   Bello, Walden (2004). Coming: A Re-Run of the 1930s? In: J. Sen, A. Anand, A. Escobar & P. Waterman (Eds.), *World Social Forum: Challenging Empires* (pp. 12–15). New Delhi: Viveka Foundation.

Document 13   Löwy, Michael (2004). Towards A New International? In: J. Sen, A. Anand, A. Escobar & P. Waterman (Eds.), *World Social Forum: Challenging Empires* (pp. 19–24). New Delhi: Viveka Foundation.

Document 14   Roy, Arundhati (2004). Confronting Empire. Speech given at the World Social Forum, Porto Alegre, January 28, 2003. In: J. Sen, A. Anand, A. Escobar & P. Waterman (Eds.), *World Social Forum: Challenging Empires* (pp. 51–54). New Delhi: Viveka Foundation.

NOTE

1. All websites were accessed last on 9 February 2017.

Index